The World's Greatest Secrets

The World's Greatest Secrets

By
ALLAN HALL

HAMLYN

Acknowledgements

The Publishers would like to thank the following organizations and
individuals for their kind permission to reproduce the illustrations
in this book:

CAMERA PRESS: 19, 111; Alan Whicker 39; MARY EVANS PICTURE LIBRARY: 34;
FRANK SPOONER PICTURES/GAMMA: 117; Tom Kasser 156/Peter Tatiner 101 /
Christian Yioujard 54L&R: JOHN FROST HISTORICAL NEWSPAPER: 128; ROBERT
HUNT LIBRARY: 59, 96; THE KEYSTONE COLLECTION: 132; NOVA SCOTIA
TOURIST BOARD: 143; Taro Yamasaki/PEOPLE WEEKLY © 1986 Time Inc.: 27;
THE PHOTOGRAPHERS LIBRARY: 149; POPPERFOTO: 78; REX FEATURES: 86, 123;
SYNDICATION INTERNATIONAL: 9; TOPHAM PICTURE LIBRARY: 65L&R, 91;
UPI/BETTMAN NEWSPHOTOS: 136, 139; THE WASHINGTON POST: 75.

Frontispiece photographs: Fatty Arbuckle, Group Captain Townsend and
Princess Margaret, two members of the Tonton Macoutes

First published in 1994 by Hamlyn, a division of
Octopus Publishing Group Limited

This 1997 edition published by Chancellor Press, an imprint of
Bounty Books, a division of Octopus Publishing Group Limited,

2-4 Heron Quays, London E14 4JP

An Hachette Livre UK Company

Reprinted 1999, 2002, 2003, 2005, 2006 (twice), 2007

ISBN: 978-1-851528-67-7

A CIP record for this book is available from the British Library

Printed and bound in Great Britain by Mackays of Chatham

Contents

CHAPTER ONE
Crime Secrets   7

CHAPTER TWO
State Secrets   37

CHAPTER THREE
Secrets of the Heart   61

CHAPTER FOUR
Military Secrets   89

CHAPTER FIVE
Secrets of Hollywood   121

CHAPTER SIX
Secrets of the Past   141

Chapter One

CRIME SECRETS

Here is a collection of murders most foul – crimes that to this day remain unsolved and where the perpetrators could still be at large – like the A1 murder – did victim Janice Weston have a secret she had to die for? Why did a dashing Guards officer sacrifice everything for the brother he loved? What was the secret of the Christmas child – a boy from nowhere whose death touched an entire community? And finally that greatest psychopath of all – Jack the Ripper – who disappeared into the London fog, never to be seen again and whose identity still remains a secret.

The Fallen Idol

Captain Simon Hayward was a member of two of the most exclusive clubs in the world – the British establishment and the Guards Regiment. Both afforded him a certain social cachet, not to mention a privileged lifestyle and a well mapped-out future. Hayward had served his country well, and the rewards of loyalty were rapid promotion in the ranks, service overseas and invitations to the best debutante balls. His masters at Wellington College in Crowthorne, in the heart of the English countryside, were proud that he had opted for military service; for generations Wellington has swelled the ranks of the British Army officer corps with fine young men. The son of an RAF officer who became a commercial airline pilot, Simon reflected that his father, had he still been alive, would have been proud of his service in the Household Division. He would have been prouder still to have seen his son astride a magnificent cavalry horse guarding the home of the Monarch – Buckingham Palace. Still, even though his father was dead, his mother Hazel had enough pride in her heart for the whole family, and never failed to positively glow whenever she mentioned the achievements of her warrior son.

Simon had two brothers, David and Christopher. David was the youngest of the three and shared Simon's traditional values. Christopher, the eldest, was the exact opposite. At school he performed badly, irrating the very same masters who were impressed by his brother's academic prowess. One classmate branded him a 'flash Harry, a loudmouth, a show off.' He left school in 1968, aged eighteen, and hit the Hippy Trail, trod by thousands of disillusioned young men and women, who walked off to the orient in search of drugs, free love, mysticism – but mostly themselves. He journeyed to Afghanistan, Thailand and India, dabbling in the mind-bending drugs favoured in the 1960s, and finally ended up on the Spanish island of Ibiza. In 1971, the island had not developed into the steel-and-glass holiday resort favoured now by package holiday Britons. Christopher made his first home in the village of Santa Gertrudis, and later near San Carlos, on a remote headland on the north of the island. Here he met a community of hippies and dropouts who had an interest in marijuana. He also found a little work ferrying day-trippers around on a boat he had just bought.

Christopher came back to London in 1972, when, on 12 August, he married Chantal Heubi at Fulham Registry Office. Chantal was a student, a

Captain Hayward in happier days before his arrest.

girl with an impeccable background. She was Swiss-born, and she and
Christopher had been lovers for two years. Christopher was then twenty-one
and almost became a father the previous spring – but Chantal lost the baby.
The marriage was unorthodox, the couple favouring the flamboyant red
robes which the mysterious 'Bhagwan' cult members wore. The marriage
lasted two years, long enough for Chantal to leave Ibiza to give birth to a son,
Tarik, back in Switzerland. Chantal kept the baby, but returned to Ibiza to
live and she and Christopher parted but remained friends.

The innocent child could not know that he would become a pawn in a sinister power play that would, eventually, destroy his uncle and force his father into the life of a fugitive.

With the sons carving out their totally different lives, Mrs Hayward was happy that the brothers at least retained a mutual respect and liking for each other. Although worlds apart in the lifestyles they pursued, Christopher was protective of his 'kid' brother, while Simon stuck up for his brother's right to live the way he saw fit. In March 1987, after Simon had completed a long, arduous tour of duty in Northern Ireland — much of his time spent on perilous covert missions with the elite SAS Regiment — he opted for a holiday in the sun in Ibiza.

Simon's days were spent drinking wine and lazing on the beaches his nights partying in the local discos and nightclubs. It was perfect rest and relaxation after the harrowing months in Ulster. But did Simon know that his brother's catamaran *Truelove* was used for more than running idle rich tourists around the islands? Did he know what the police already knew — that Christopher was a lynchpin of a top smuggling organization which dealt in marijuana from Morocco, landed it in Ibiza and processed it in Spain before filtering it out to the lucrative European markets? Was he aware that *Truelove* had sailed for years to the Moroccan town of M'diq, where Christopher loaded its hull with cannabis resin? Simon always claimed he never knew anything of his brother's criminal activities.

Midway through the first week of March, Simon then thirty-three, agreed to do his brother a favour. Sandra Agar, his attractive, well-bred London girlfriend had flown home, so he had time on his hands. He would drive Christopher's XJ6 British racing green Jaguar to Sweden where his brother assured him he had a buyer already arranged to purchase it. The car, he told Simon, was a nuisance, not built for the twisting roads and back lanes of Ibiza — especially the pitted dirt road on the island's northern tip which led to his new home. 'Would you drive it back across the European mainland and sell it for me?', he asked. It was an offer Simon jumped at.

Nearly 1,800 miles away in Stockholm the snow still lay on the ground from the bitter winter. Police officers from the city's narcotics squad and Uppsala, Sweden's main university town fifty miles away, were meeting to discuss details of a drug-busting operation that they had been planning for two years.

Uppsala is outwardly one of Sweden's loveliest cities, but there is also a seamy side to the place — drug peddling. With its 5,000 strong university population — plus all the fringe elements and meeting places which serve that population — there was a ready-made market for narcotics peddling. The narcotics squad in Stockholm had been monitoring the drug organization which smuggled the cannabis in from Spain for two years. Christopher

Hayward did not know it, but he had been under surveillance for months. All the police were waiting for was the chance to catch a courier when the drugs were being delivered, thereby ensnaring him, the consignment and hopefully, at the very least, disrupting the flow of drugs for months. It could also, hoped the detectives, lead to the arrest of further gang members – maybe even to the dismantling of the network. All they were waiting for was the next consignment . . . and intelligence told them that it was due in March.

The Jaguar snaked through the Pyrenees, up through Bordeaux, around Paris, on up through Belgium, Holland, Germany, Denmark and finally purred to a halt to catch the ferry across to Sweden. Simon Hayward was on the final leg of his journey – to meet a man in a railway station at Linkoping, 120 miles south of Stockholm. The rendezvous was at ten o'clock at night and the man he was assigned to meet was called Lokesh – a friend of his brother's from Ibiza whom he had briefly met once on the island. He did not know then, he later claimed, that the man who climbed into the front seat of the Jaguar was actually a long-time drug peddler called Forbes Cay Mitchell. Cay Mitchell told him to drive to a house where they would stay – in reality the 'drop' house for the drug consignment. But waiting in the shadows was an armed squad of the Stockholm narcotics team that had planned the operation to ensnare the organization's courier. It was Friday, 13 March 1987 and the day could not have been more unlucky for Simon Hayward. Inspector Jan Bihlar walked over to the window after Simon's car was pulled over and with full courtesy, told the man who had guarded Her Majesty Queen Elizabeth the Second that he was under arrest.

In Uppsala, where Hayward was first taken, the car was put into a police garage. It did not take the specialized drug-busting team long to discover that hidden in the hollows of the Jaguar's doors were 50·5 kilos of high grade cannabis resin, worth over £250,000 at street value. Pictures taken of Captain Hayward alongside the car with Swedish prosecutor Ulf Forsberg, who would be handling the case, seemed to show a man completely dumb-founded, numb with shock and surprise. Captain Hayward, who flashed his Army identification card at the police when he was apprehended, was charged with being a courier of the drug consignment and charged with smuggling the cannabis in the certain knowledge that he would be paid £20,000 for his trouble. He was then led away to the cells as Fleet Street newspapers despatched reporters to Sweden for the sensational story – the story of a man duped by his own brother; a modern-day Cain and Abel, with a fate worse than death for the officer who now faced disgrace, humiliation and punishment.

11

It was police Inspector Jan-Erik Nilson who first briefed the hungry pressmen with the facts. In an upstairs room of Uppsala police station, usually reserved for lectures and operation planning, he told them how Christopher Hayward had been 'fingered' by another member of the drugs syndicate, Forbes Cay Mitchell. Aberdeen-born Cay Mitchell, a committed marijuana smoker, was netted by the police at the same time, he explained. In exchange for leniency, he told the police that he had been involved in many shipments of cannabis to Sweden; and that he had been in Ibiza when Simon was there with his brother. He heard them talking about the plot to get the drugs into the country via the compartments in the Jaguar. Simon was needed because the regular courier, known only as Macundo, was getting jittery and worn down after one mission too many. Simon, he said, was a willing conspirator, lured into the international drug smuggling network by greed and excitement.

One man would have freed Captain Hayward – but it would of course have ended his own liberty. That man was his wayward brother Christopher. He vanished into Europe, covering his tracks. He has not been seen since. But the manner of his disappearance – and the mysterious death of his ex-wife Chantal three months after Simon's arrest – have led to immense speculation about the whole sinister affair which led to the terrible downfall of an officer and a gentleman.

Police said initially they hoped to make telephone contact with Christopher within days. They believed he might want to cut the same kind of deal that Cay Mitchell had done – leniency in return for co-operation. But Hayward was on the run – a fugitive not only from the law but from the menacing, ruthless figures who controlled the drugs syndicate.

A newspaper managed to confirm that while Interpol was searching for Hayward, he had docked *Truelove*, his 57 feet catamaran in M'diq, where he had a secret reunion with his son Tarik. Later there were phone calls to London from Christopher to his mother – in which he said if he gave himself up for questioning he would be killed. More seriously, so would Tarik. He could not come forward to speak for Simon. For him, there was no hope. Cay Mitchell, at his trial before Hayward's, said it was a plot which the Captain was fully aware of; that it was a challenge to him and that he would be handsomely rewarded for his efforts. For his evidence, Cay Mitchell was given a seven year jail term.

Lawyers for Simon prepared his case – but the circumstantial evidence was incriminating. Why a secret rendezvous in a windswept railway station car-park so late at night? Why was a screwdriver which fitted into specially-designed holes to prise off the door covers from the inside found in the car? What about the overheard conversation testified to by Cay Mitchell in which he alleged Simon was a willing participant in the scheme? All Simon

Hayward could argue was that he was an innocent dupe – a pawn in a power game which his brother had manipulated for greed. He steadfastly maintained his innocence, but a judge and jury found him guilty and sentenced him to five years. Even with the news of the sentence there was still no sign of Christopher anywhere.

Shortly before the verdict, in July 1987 Chantal, Christopher's ex-wife, telephoned from Ibiza to Mrs Hayward at her London home, to say she knew who was behind the drugs run – 'and that it was not Simon or Christopher.' She intended to fly to London and speak with solicitors to give her evidence and testify in the court hearing at Stockholm if necessary. But only days before she was scheduled to arrive, she was found dead – an autopsy had revealed a massive drug overdose, injected into the arm with a needle. What was mystifying was that Chantal had experimented with marijuana, but had never taken hard drugs. There was no evidence on her skin that she was a hardened junkie – just one small pin-prick. And the needle mark was on her left arm – and she was left handed. It raised the question: why did a girl who had never injected herself before use her unfamiliar right hand to pump a lethal cocktail of drugs into her left arm? And why did this occur just days before she was to give evidence to help out her ex-brother-in-law? Christopher Hayward remains on the run. Is he the keeper of a secret which damned his brother? Did he dupe him, or were they partners in crime? What is the terrible power of the organization that he once worked for which has sentenced him, as much as justice sentenced his brother, to a life with no hiding place? Simon Hayward has taken his punishment like a man, although he is stripped of rank, has been discharged from the Army, and had to linger in jail while his mother buried her youngest son, David, who was tragically killed in a car crash in January 1988.

Sweden is a democratic country with decent laws and a judiciary based on equality and fairness. But from his prison cell, Simon Hayward said: 'Ninety-nine per cent of me believes that Christopher stitched me up. Only that other one per cent clings to the fact that he is my brother, that he couldn't have done. But ninety-nine per cent screams out that he did.

'One thing is very obvious; whether he did or he didn't, whether he is genuinely terrified of something or somebody I know nothing about, there *must* have been some way for him to get a message or information through to clear me. He has not done that, and for that I will never forgive him.'

The A1 Murder

Did Janice Weston know a secret that she had to die for? It is a question that has baffled lawmen since the morning of 11 September 1983 when her badly battered body was found dumped in a ditch next to a lay-by on the A1 Great North Road. The frenzied attacker had clubbed her repeatedly around the head with a blunt instrument – police were later to discover it was the jack from her own car – and had thrown her body into the water-filled ditch. David Hurst, a cyclist who had stopped to rest in the lay-by on the northbound section of the road near Huntingdon, Cambridgeshire, raised the alarm, triggering a murder probe which remains unsolved to this day.

Janice Weston was a brilliant lawyer, a product of convent school education who had attained a degree in law from Manchester University. She was well liked, cheerful, pretty, and charming – a woman of the 1980s who had everything to live for.

Janice Weston graduated while in her mid-twenties and quickly landed a plum job in the slect London law firm of Oppenheimer, Nathan and Vandyk. While she was there, Janice met the two most important men in her life – one was Tony Weston, who was destined to become her husband. The other was Heinz Isner, a refugee from Hitler's Germany who had come to London before the outbreak of World War Two and made a fortune from merchant banking. Isner was forty-one years older than Janice, and fell in love with her. But while she remained fond of the old gentleman – who once, in an old fashioned, courteous way, asked if she would be his bride – her affections were for Tony Weston, an ambitious property developer. While he became her lover, she never forgot the gracious old gentleman who settled for being her escort on trips to the ballet and London's West End theatres.

Janice specialized in computer law just at the time that the microchip revolution was thrusting business, financial and industrial life from the Victorian era to the modern age. Word processors would be in every office within a decade and the vast network of computers and their useage would require new laws every step of the way. That was her field and she excelled in it. She was recognized for her talents and employed in 1976 by the top practice of Charles Russell and Company, as a partner.

She was well paid for her work and dealt at the highest levels with clients and management. A year after her appointment the kindly Heinz Isner died.

Janice had realized that he was an amicable old fellow and she had responded to his affections with dignity and courtesy, only too willing to be the friend he was obviously seeking. It was only with his death that she realized the price that he put on her friendship – a legacy of close on £145,000 of paintings, money, stocks and shares and antiques from his vast estate. Janice Weston, was now financially secure in her own right thanks to the legacy and her meticulous attention to detail at work which earned her both promotion and the money which went with it. Her boss Lord Nathan was later to remark that she was 'one of the most brilliant corporate lawyers I have ever known.'

It wasn't until 1982, after Tony Weston was divorced from his first wife, that Janice and he were free to marry. The pair combined business with pleasure – Janice investing some of her money into apartments at a mansion called Clopton Manor in Northamptonshire which property dealer Tony suggested would be a good buy. They used one of the apartments as a weekend retreat when away from their home in London's Holland Park.

Tony Weston was successful too; his business deals brought him an enviable lifestyle as he dealt in property in both England and Europe. When he and Janice were up at Clopton Manor they often drank in the local pubs and were liked by everyone for their quiet, restrained manner.

In 1983 Janice set herself a new task, researching and writing a book on computer law and the latest safeguards for business and commerce in using new technology. In September she was still working on the book when Tony Weston went to France to negotiate the purchase of a Loire Valley chateau. He was never to see his wife again.

On 10 September 1983 Janice was at home doing research on her book. Later that day, at 5.00pm, she turned up at the law offices where she worked – police were later to interview a colleague who testified that she was there. What happened to Janice after that is a mixture of mystery, conjecture and speculation. The next time she was seen was the following morning by the cyclist in the lonely A1 lay-by, fourteen miles from Clopton Manor.

Among the first on the scene on that Sunday morning was Detective Chief Superintendent Len Bradley, Cambridgeshire's head of CID. The first, and most puzzling thing about the appalling crime was: how did Janice get there? For there was no sign of her car. She was not in fact identified for another forty eight hours, when law firm colleagues alerted her sister, who in turn alerted police about her absence. Twenty-four hours after they identified Janice, an alert policeman spotted, abandoned, in the Camden Town area of London, Janice's car – with bloodstains over the window and dashboard. At the scene, a search of the field which bordered the road revealed the car jack – the murder weapon, according to a Home Office pathologist.

Len Bradley, a dedicated, ultra-professional policeman with many years' experience, had to find out why this professional, thirty-six-year-old woman was murdered in an anonymous lay-by on one of Britain's busiest trunk roads; why there was no sign of a robbery at the scene or of sexual assault; why the killer stole her car and drove it to London; why she had driven north in the first place. There were plenty of questions but no answers.

Detectives despatched to the Holland Park address found the remains of a half-eaten meal and a single wine glass, indicating that she had dined alone. They were curious as to why the house had the appearance that she had left in a hurry – the normally fastidious Janice had not done the washing up and had left with her purse, but not her handbag; usually a possession that women never left behind. In the face of too-few clues, the police reasoned this: that Janice Weston was telephoned, or received a message by some other means, that necessitated her driving up the A1 towards Clopton Manor. Was she, then, lured to the lay-by by that person for an appointment with death?

One of the most bizarre aspects of the case, and one which has still not been cleared up, was the mystery of the number plates. Forty-eight hours before the murder was revealed to the Press, a man walked into a car spares shop in Royston, Hertfordshire, and ordered two spare number plates – with the same registration as Janice's Alfa Romeo car. The mystery man has never been traced. Police looked to the car for clues. They discovered that on the Saturday morning before Janice's ill fated journey, she had collected a repaired tyre which had her husband's name and telephone number scrawled on the side in yellow water-resistant chalk. The repairman put it into the boot, leaving the spare on the car. However, when the vehicle was found in London, the repaired tyre was back on the car and the spare was missing. It was, mused police, entirely plausible that Janice had had a blow-out and stopped to change the wheel in the lay-by when her attacker struck her with repeated blows from the jack. But why would the spare wheel be missing?

Tony Weston came back from France and pleaded with the public for information about his wife's killer. To cover all angles, detectives were sent to the Loire Valley to investigate Mr Weston's movements on the weekend that his wife was so cruelly murdered. He was held in custody for fifty-five hours in December and a report was prepared for the Director of Public Prosecutions, but there were no charges.

Police satisfied themselves that Janice Weston was not racing off for an illicit liaison with a lover; she was not given to affairs of the heart. There was no sign that she had picked up a crazed hitch-hiker or any reason to suppose that a madman would lurk in that particular lay-by on a freezing night.

Was she, as one theory suggested 'silenced' because her work in computers touched on high-tech espionage – or worse? Why Janice Weston had to die, when she was at the pinnacle of her career, is still, sadly, a secret.

The Missing Earl

He did it – English law in the form of a coroner's jury decreed that Lord Lucan killed his children's nanny on that dark winter's night. The Edwardian-looking Earl with a penchant for gambling and a disdain for modern life wielded the hammer that killed pretty Sandra Rivett. But what has puzzled policemen hunting for him ever since the murder in November 1974, has been the secret of what happened to him. Is he dead? Is he alive? More importantly, do his friends know his fate? Perhaps even the most outrageous theory of all is that he is innocent and took to the life of a fugitive because no one would ever believe otherwise. What are the secrets of Lord Lucan?

The story starts, of course, with the murder; when a panic stricken Lady Veronica Lucan ran from her home in the pouring rain to a local pub and yelled to the astonished drinkers: 'Murder, there's been a murder. He murdered the nanny.' On Lady Veronica's head was an extremely deep wound which poured blood, mingling with the rain running down her face and into her nightclothes.

Officers forced their way into the home at 46 Lower Belgrave Street where they found the lower half of the mews in darkness. Police Sergeant Donald Baker, directed by the light of his torch, saw, at the end of the stairs leading to the basement, smears of what looked like blood on the wallpaper. Gritting his teeth, he advanced further. The police then made their way upstairs where they found the Lucan children. After comforting them the police officers went to the basement. There, on the hard floor, in a canvas Post Office mailbag, was the body of Sandra Rivett.

The murder weapon was found half-an-hour later – a nine-inch, two and a quarter pound length of lead piping wrapped in medical plaster. Lady Frances Lucan, the eldest child, ten years old, told police that she had been watching TV with her mother in the main bedroom when Sandra went downstairs to make some hot drinks. She was gone twenty minutes when Lady Lucan spoke with Frances and told her to watch the TV alone while she checked on what had happened to the nanny. She reappeared with a wound on her head ... with her husband, Lord Lucan. It was the last time that little Lady Frances ever saw him.

Lady Lucan, in hospital after her ordeal, told police this story; that she found the half-landing in darkness when she went to search for the nanny.

17

She called out Sandra's name and there was no reply, she then heard a noise in the cloakroom behind her. She turned – and then a gloved hand grasped her throat and a rain of blows were delivered to her head. Panicking, she said she grabbed the attacker by his genitals and squeezed hard. The man forced her to the ground and tried to gouge out her eyes – releasing the pressure, as the pain from Lady's Lucan's grip forced him backwards. She said she looked up and saw the face of her husband.

Lady Lucan claimed he told her that he had killed the nanny, mistakenly thinking it was her. She said she saved her own life by reasoning with him that she would help him to get away. They went upstairs to a bedroom and she lay down on the bed while he went to find some wet towels to bathe her wounds. 'While he was gone I got up and dashed out of the house,' said Lady Lucan. That was her frantic dash to the pub which signalled the beginning of one of history's most intriguing murder cases.

Later that first night, 7 November, Lucan's mother, the Dowager Countess Lucan, arrived at the house to meet the police. She said that her son had telephoned, asking her to be there. She told detectives that he had said a 'terrible catastrophe' had occurred, in which his wife Veronica and the nanny Sanda had been hurt by an intruder whom he had disturbed. It was his mother who revealed the first of many secrets about the mysterious Earl. She informed the officers that her son and Lady Veronica had separated and the children were wards of court. Many of Lucan's friends were unaware of this because the outward appearance of a conservative, family man was one he both nurtured and cherished.

Checks at the nearby flat he kept and another mews home which was his did not reveal any clues about his whereabouts or what had gone on earlier that evening. Police found Lord Lucan's passport in his flat together with a suit that was laid out on the bed as if he was meaning to pack it. But from the way the evidence was shaping up, it seemed as if Lady Lucan's story was true; the police began to think that Lucan had bludgeoned the nanny to death after mistaking her for his wife. Sandra Rivett, twenty-nine, died because she did not take the usual evening off – the evening that Lucan presumed she would not be in in the house.

Police began to chip away at the facade of the Earl who behaved as if he belonged in another century. Outwardly he displayed all the signs of a privileged life, with his fine homes, live-in nanny, membership of gentlemen's clubs, a Mercedes car and Savile Row suits in the wardrobe. He was a high-roller on the backgammon and card tables of private gambling clubs where his considerable prowess with the cards earned him the nickname of 'Lucky' among his friends. It was not unusual for 'Lucky' to scoop £5,000 in an afternoon of gambling at the tables of his most exclusive club, the

Lord 'Lucky' Lucan in his ceremonial robes.

Clermont, in London. He held bank accounts in Rhodesia and the Bahamas, and was generally reckoned to be financially sound, having inherited family funds, as well as silver and land in Ireland when he succeeded to the title of Earl of Lucan in January 1964. But Lucan's outwardly affluent lifestyle was, police learned, not quite as financially sound as it seemed.

Lucan had frittered away much of the money. He had a fixed annual income of £7,000 per annum from a trust fund and spent large sums in legal fees in his bid to gain custody of his children in a court case in January 1973. At one stage he was spending £400 a week on a private detective to watch his wife's home as he hoped to find illicit liaisons which might convince a judge that the youngsters would be better off under his wing. Another time, his beloved Clermont club in London's ritzy Berkeley Square once withdrew his credit facilities for a time because he bounced a cheque there for £10,000. In short, Lord Lucan was going broke, and was being eaten away with an almost pathological hatred of his wife which, police surmised, he thought he could exorcise with a swift, clean simple murder.

Police began to trace his movements prior to the killing and the attack on Lady Lucan. The night before he had dined with forty other people at a formal dinner. The day of the murder itself he had lunch with friends at the Clermont, met a literary agent to talk over an article he was planning for a magazine on gambling, and at around 8.30 p.m. phoned the Clermont to book a table for four people for dinner.

He arrived at the club some sixteen minutes later, spoke with the doorman, and then drove off. His guests arrived but he – the host – was never seen again.

On the Saturday morning, 9 November, police discovered that Lucan had posted two letters to his friend, millionaire amateur jockey Bill Shand Kydd. The letters were postmarked Uckfield, Sussex, and had blood on the envelopes. One read: 'Dear Bill, the most ghastly circumstances arose tonight, which I have described briefly to my mother when I interrupted the fight at Lower Belgrave Street and the man left.

'V (for Veronica) accused me of having hired him. I took her upstairs and sent Frances to bed and tried to clean her up. She lay doggo for a bit. I went into the bathroom and left the house.

'The circumstantial evidence against me is strong in that V will say it was all my doing and I will lie doggo for a while, but I am only concerned about the children. If you can manage it I would like them to live with you. V has demonstrated her hatred for me in the past and would like to see me accused. For George (his son) and Frances to go through life knowing their father had been accused of attempted murder would be too much for them.

'When they are old enough to understand explain to them the dream of paranoia and look after them.' He signed himself 'Lucky'.

The second letter carried the heading 'financial matters' and outlined a sale at Christie's he had arranged for family silver.

Finally police spoke with Susan Maxwell Scott at the estate she shared with her husband, Ian Maxwell Scott, on the outskirts of Uckfield – the place where the letters had been posted from. Lord Lucan had told them the same story as the one he recounted to his mother – that he had gone into the home to act as his wife's rescuer and found himself being accused by her of Sandra Rivett's murder. He drove away from her home at 1.15 a.m. in a dark saloon car and has never been seen again.

Or has he? Part of the unanswered enigma surrounding the Earl has been his flight. One theory put forward was that he hopped on a cross channel ferry and threw himself into the cold water from the deck of the Newhaven–Dieppe ship. Another was that he went to a private airfield and flew out of the country with a friend at the controls. Other flights of fancy suggest that he changed his identity, took the small amount of capital he had in a Swiss bank account, and set out to embark on a new life away from justice and the stigma of murder.

But Scotland Yard detectives are never satisfied with untidy ends. One of the toughest nuts to crack has been Lucan's tight circle of aristocratic friends, many of whom seemed bound to Lucan by a code of loyalty and honour rarely found in twentieth century Britain. A code, some policemen think, which may even have transcended society's most heinous crime – murder. One source close to the investigation once said that he believed that up to five of Lucan's friends know that he hadn't taken the coward's way out and killed himself. The obvious suggestion is that Lucan's friends, an elite mafia of the rich and privileged, kept his secret and somehow assisted his flight and bolstered the start of his life as a fugitive. It is only a theory and no one has ever been charged with aiding and abetting the flight of a wanted criminal. But in the minds of detectives who are only happy when the loose ends are tied up, it is one that comes back frequently to haunt them. Until all the answers are known, Lord Lucan's final secret remains safe.

Jack the Ripper

In 1888 the British Empire was at its zenith. The sun never set on this glorious imperial bastion which spanned the globe, embracing peoples of every race, creed and colour. But in London, the centre of this huge domain, there was a place where the sun never shone. The East End was a disgrace to the Empire and to civilized values. People lived in squalor, poverty and filth. Child deaths were double the national average and prostitution and drunkenness, sexual abuse of minors and murders, were rife. It was the sordid environment for a killer whose notoriety lives on unabated to this day. Jack the Ripper made the mean streets of the East End his killing ground. Even now, with most of the crumbling slums gone, the taverns of his day replaced with office blocks and the gas lamps ripped out in favour of electric ones, the East End has become a lurid shrine for Ripper enthusiasts, fascinated by the macabre killer's violent deeds. But the question remains: just who was Jack the Ripper? His crimes were not all that remarkable, given the catalogue of horror which man has learned to come to terms with in the twentieth century. He butchered five women, admittedly in a gruesome manner. It is the question of identity, with all the suspicions that Jack the Ripper may have been someone highly placed in British society, which has made the 'Monster of the East End' a creature of intrigue and has ensured his dastardly deeds are never far from the public's mind.

Jack the Ripper may have gone down as history's most famous murderer but his reign of terror was a short one. He first struck on 31 August 1888. Mary Ann Nichols, a prostitute who haunted the Whitechapel area of the East End plying her trade was found butchered in one of the area's many dark alleyways. 'Pretty Polly' as the forty two year old whore was known, was a chronic drunkard and well-known inhabitant of the gin palaces in the area.

Police think Mary Ann approached a tall stranger with the time-honoured 'looking for a good time, mister?' By the time the man had dragged her into the shadows, it was too late. A hand went around her throat, and in seconds she was cut from ear to ear. 'Only a madman could have done this', said a police surgeon who was to examine the body later. 'I have never seen so horrible a case. She was ripped about in a manner that only a person skilled in the use of a knife could have achieved.'

Murders in that deprived − and depraved − area were not uncommon. Police were happy to put the murder down to a single frenzied attack − until just one week later, on 8 September, 'Dark Annie' Chapman, also a prostitute, was found in Hanbury Street near Spitalfields Market with her few pitiful possessions neatly laid out alongside her disembowelled corpse. Although there was no obvious sign of rape, with this murder as with the first there was every indication that the killer was motivated by some terrible sexual rage as he cut and slashed with grotesque abandon. The dissection of 'Dark Annie', with all her entrails laid out next to the corpse, indicated a knowledge of anatomy or surgery not found in the everyday sex killer.

After the second murder, on 25 September, a mocking letter was sent to a Fleet Street news agency. It read: 'Dear Boss, I keep on hearing that the police have caught me. But they won't fix me yet. I am down on certain types of women and I won't stop ripping them until I do get buckled. Grand job, that last job was, I gave the lady no time to squeal. I love my work and want to start again. You will soon hear from me with my funny little game. I saved some of the proper stuff in a little ginger beer bottle after my last job to write with, but it went thick like glue and I can't use it. Red ink is fit enough I hope. Ha! Ha!

Next time I shall clip the ears off and send them to the police, just for jolly.'

The sick message was signed: Jack the Ripper.

Victim number three was Elizabeth Stride, nicknamed 'Long Liz' because of her height. A policeman found the body of forty four year old Liz in Berner's Street, Whitechapel, on 30 September near some factory gates. Like the others her throat had been cut from behind, but she did not suffer mutilation or sexual savagery. This led police to think that the murderer had been disturbed in his gruesome work – for on the same day they discovered victim number four a few streets away in Mitre Square. Catherine Eddowes, forty-three, was disembowelled and her face practically hacked off.

By the time of this fourth murder, Ripper hysteria had gripped London and was raging faster than the plague in the dark, damp passageways of the East End. Women began arming themselves with knives and whistles to attract the police; the *Illustrated Police News* speculated that well-to-do ladies were arming themselves with pearly-handled pistols in case the Ripper was tempted to move up the social scale in his search for bloody satisfaction.

The Eddowes murder disturbed the police greatly. Her body was by far the most mutilated of all the victims and there was a trail of blood leading to a wall where, scrawled in chalk, was the message: 'The Jewes are not men to be blamed for nothing.' Sir Charles Warren, the head of the Metropolitan Police Force personally removed the notice – and thereby may have destroyed some vital evidence. He was concerned that with the influx into the area of Jews from Eastern Europe – and racial tensions already beginning to bubble – this note could have led to savage reprisals.

The rumours about who the murderer was circulated like wildfire. Some of the frightened wretches who lived in the East End said it was a policeman on his nightly rounds, his job giving him the perfect alibi to be out at night on those cold, dark streets. One suspect was a Russian-born doctor called Michael Ostrog, rumour having it that he was sent by the Tsarist secret police to stir up hatred against the expatriate Jews who fled Russia from persecution; others that it was a mad surgeon, or even Sir Charles Warren himself – a leading freemason who removed the notice to protect a freemason killer.

The final death came on 9 November when Mary Kelly, aged 25 and also a prostitute, was grotesquely mutilated in her squalid rented home. On the morning of 10 November Henry Bowers, her landlord, knocked on her door to collect unpaid rent. The previous evening the attractive blonde girl had been seen approaching strangers asking them for cash. The last one she approached – tall, dark, with a moustache and a deerstalker hat – was her killer. Bowers saw the remains of Mary and later told police: 'I shall be haunted by this for the rest of my life.'

Mary's death was to be the last. One hundred years later, the puzzle of the Ripper's bloody but brief reign has still not been solved. It was with the passage of time that more and more people grew intrigued by the Ripper mystery. One suspect who has continued to cause violent debate was Queen Victoria's grandson Prince Albert Victor, Duke of Clarence. The finger was pointed at him because he was said to be mad, incarcerated in a mental institution after he had committed the murders because the scandal would have been too great had it ever been revealed to the world.

However, Inspector Robert Sagar, who played a leading part in the Ripper investigation, said before his death in 1924: 'We had good reason to suspect a man who lived in Butcher's Row, Aldgate. We watched him carefully. There was no doubt that this man was insane. After a time his friends thought it advisable to have him removed to a private asylum. After he was removed there were no more Ripper atrocities.'

Another prime suspect is one favoured by several authors, namely Montagu John Druitt, whose body was found floating in the Thames a few weeks after the murder of Mary Kelly. In their book *The Ripper Legacy*, authors Martin Howells and Keith Skinner say that this impoverished barrister was the man that the police of the day reckoned to be the guilty party. They point to the fact that after his death there were no more Ripper murders. But those writers who favour the Duke of Clarence are swift to point out that there were no more slayings after he was incarcerated. Nevertheless, Druitt's family had a history of mental illness and he had acquired basic medical skills as a young man. The arguments rage unabated.

John Stalker, who retired last year as Deputy Chief Constable of Greater

Manchester, delved into the Ripper files and declared: 'There is still not a shred of real evidence sufficient for a court of law against anyone. The truth is that Jack the Ripper was never in danger of capture. The police, I am certain, came nowhere near him.

'The Metropolitan Police of 1888 were dealing with something quite new: The first recognized series of sexual murders committed by a man who was a stranger to his victims. And 100 years on those are still the most difficult crimes of all to investigate.'

The Christmas Child

Chuck Kleveland was armed with his twelve-bore shotgun and had his western-style jacket buttoned up against the cold as he stepped out in the frozen morning air to hunt for elusive pheasants in his native Chester, Nebraska. It was Christmas Eve and Chuck, forty-four, who ran a truck-stop diner had closed his business for the festivities. He was actually driving from Chester to nearby Hebron to get his 'holiday haircut' as he termed it, but driving down the back roads afforded him ample chance of potting a bird for the Yuletide table. He stuffed extra ammunition in his fleece-lined pockets, jumped behind the wheel of his pick-up, turned on the engine which belched blue-smoke in the frosty air and lurched down the rutted backroad to Chuck's appointment with the barber.

Chuck Kleveland was scanning the horizon hungrily for the birds that would make a tasty treat for his wife's table, when his eye was caught by a flash of blue. He noticed it because it stood out so starkly in the four-feet high grass, tipped with white frost. Chuck backed up the truck – and then rubbed his eyes in disbelief. At first he thought it was a discarded mannequin, a tailor's dummy tossed in the long grass by a thoughtless adult, or the toy of a child. But it was neither. It was the body of a young boy. Chuck was not to know how deeply this discovery was going to affect him in the days to come.

Chuck scrambled through the long grass to the lifeless bundle that was prostrate just fifteen feet from the cab of his pick-up. 'I thought it was a joke or something' he says now, still reeling in disbelief from those first awful moments when reality was sinking in. 'I thought it was a doll, a dummy. It scared the life out of me when I realized it was a child.'

Clad in a one-piece pyjama suit, the child was lying flat on his back, his face fixed serenely as if he had passed away without pain. One hand was lying flat on his chest, across his heart, almost, said Kleveland, as if it had been placed there in a gesture by the killer. The child was just over four feet in height, with blond hair, a gap in his front teeth and freckles. Altogether, thought Kleveland fighting back the panic rising in him, a rather endearing face.

He ran back to the pick-up. Like most drivers in this back-of-beyond region, he had a CB radio in the cab. Using the emergency channel, he called his secretary and told her to contact the local sheriff. When the emergency summons went out over the police radio, Sheriff Gary Young, initially thought it was a pre-Christmas prank by some rednecks who had partaken of too much good cheer. 'A dead body found abandoned in Thayer County?' he said. 'The prospect just didn't seem real.' As an eight-year veteran of the Sheriff's department he had spent his time in the force breaking up brawls and probing some petty break-ins. Homicide was a big city crime.

Young raced to the scene after being convinced of the authenticity of the call. He was emotionally choked when he bent over and looked at the tranquil features of the little boy. Kleveland saw on a second look that part of the boy's nose and upper lip had been eaten away – probably by mice, he thought. But there was no sign of a violent struggle or a gaping wound; nothing to suggest why the little boy had got into this field, in this way to be discovered on 24 December 1985.

The body of the boy was taken to a funeral home in Hebron where several police investigators from the state capital of Lincoln examined him. Strangely, they found no evidence of foul play. They checked the listings for runaways, local orphanages where children, spurred by a seasonal desire to see their real parents, or try to find them, often made a break. They drew a blank. But many enquiries simply could not be answered – it was Christmas, and like most places the season of goodwill meant that offices were shut and phones rang unanswered. The officials of Hebron decided to wrap the child up in his clothes and attend to his pathetic corpse after the holiday. The little boy was placed in the town mortuary and Hebron settled down to extremely muted Christmas celebrations.

There is no doubt that the dead child haunted Thayer County's Christmas. News of the grim find spread rapidly throughout the rural community and sparked more than one frantic search for a missing child or a son unreturned from a family errand. The close-knit farming communities which made up

LITTLE BOY
ABANDONED
FOUND NEAR
CHESTER, NEB.
DEC. 24, 1985

'The Christmas Child' is laid to rest.

Hebron and Chester only numbered some 7,000 people, so it was natural that it became the topic of conversation in every home. The locals also gave the boy a name – The Christmas Child.

Chuck Kleveland felt the tragedy more than most. He had found the little boy and it cast a darker shadow over his home than others. His daughter Amy, eighteen, couldn't even bother to fake a Christmas spirit. 'I felt very strange on Christmas day,' she said. 'I couldn't celebrate anything. I felt there was nothing to be cheery about. I thought of this little boy who wouldn't be opening any presents on Christmas morning and that made me cry.' For others, the child's death coming on Christmas Eve signified much deeper religious meanings and sparked many different emotions. The Reverend Jean Samuelson, pastor of Chester's United Methodist Church said: 'There is an aura about it. Why did God send us a child on Christmas Eve?'

For the police, there was nothing quite so metaphysical about it. They had questions to answer, a puzzle to solve. Who was this boy? Why was he here, why was he dead, how did he die? Sheriff Young through that he would have the case solved in a few days. He could not have been more wrong, for in his office to this day the file sits – unsolved. 'I never thought it would turn out as case unsolved,' he says reflectively.

The routine work was done – descriptions of the boy were sent out across the state, then further afield, to social services agencies, police departments and child welfare groups. The autopsy on the child revealed a small one-inch birthmark inside his right calf, and a small circular scar on his right forearm. The FBI computer in Washington was tapped into, cross-checking against all children who had gone missing in the United States for that year and the year before. Over 200 leads and tips of 'possibles' were followed up, but they came to nothing. 'What really bothered me in those first few weeks was that a little child could just vanish, just shuffle off,' said Young.

The autopsy revealed little else, though. Because the boy's body had been frozen in the sub-zero temperatures, the blood tests were inconclusive. The pathologist pinpointed the date of death as 23 December, but he could not centre on the cause. The boy had not died of natural causes – but there were no signs of stabbing, shooting, strangulation or poisoning, apart from a slightly higher than normal trace of carbon monoxide present. The theory which was settled on what that the child was suffocated until he lost consciousness and was then placed outside in the cold with his hand placed over his heart, ready to die in the low temperatures. 'I could never accept that this was anything short of homicide' said County Attorney Dan Werner. 'If I believed the boy died of natural causes after the parents left him I would not be pursuing this.'

So why did the Christmas Child have to die? Slowly it began to circulate that perhaps the boy held some dark secret against an adult – the witness to a murder, perhaps, or the eavesdropper on a criminal plot which had ultimately led to his death. The mystery now obsesses the townsfolk. Thoughts of the boy appeared in the journals of the High School teenagers kept by students at the Chester Hubbell Byron High School. 'Nobody knew this child and yet he has touched all of us', wrote one teenager, Carl Kristienson. 'What had he done that he had to die for it? Is there someone bad in our community? What is the reason – will we ever know?' 'He wasn't just dumped here,' said Sheriff Young, 'he was carefully placed. Someone picked this spot to be his last. But why, why, why?'

Slowly the people of King County realized that the little boy had become part of their souls. They even gave him a name – Matthew – which means 'gift of God'. An undertaker's firm donated a coffin and another firm supplied a headstone and so on Friday 21 March 1986 the boy was laid to rest in the small Chester cemetery, his marble headstone bearing the inscription: 'Little boy found abandoned near Chester, Neb., 24 December 1985.' The Reverend Samuelson conducted the funeral service, and told mourners: 'We all know the names of little ones who have died, but this one has no name. He haunted us, he haunted me personally. I asked in prayer, "Lord, why do you keep speaking to me about this child? Why should I feel guilt?" The answer: "He has been in your life in other forms, and you have not heard him or seen him because you were too busy trying to prove yourself worth." That is the young boy's message.'

Dan Werner is too long in the tooth as a lawman to pin the reason for the child's death on some spiritual message. He understands that the townspeople's souls have been salved with the word that some form of divine reasoning may have been behind the boy's tragic demise, but he is having none of it. He said: 'Funerals are for the living, and this one makes the people in the area feel better because they have a personal relationship with him; they have kind of adopted him. But his death still tugs at me; I want to solve it.'

The Green River Killer

Police say he could be anyone. He could be a doctor, a lawyer, a car repairer, a shoe salesman. He could be sitting next to you as your read this and he will walk away out of your life without a word passed or a glance exchanged. But his secret is the darkest one yet to be discovered in American criminal history – for he is the Green River Killer, a demonic monster who makes the Yorkshire Ripper look like an amateur apprentice and has, so far, ruthlessly accounted for the lives of at least 42 women. The secret of his success, say detectives, is that he is so ordinary....

It was back in July 1982 that two little boys were out on a fishing trip along the Green River – a stretch of water which meanders slowly near the Seattle–Tacoma Airport in Washington state. The children were bicycling along with their fishing gear, intent on an afternoon of fun by the river, when they made the discovery. One of the boys saw what he thought was a log floating in the shallows, near the iron girders of Peck Bridge. He waded in and rolled it towards himself with his foot before reeling back in horror. He had found the body of sixteen year old Wendy Coffield, the first known victim of the Green River Killer.

Over the next weeks, months, years, Green River's good name – which for generations had signified peace, tranquillity and beauty, was gone forever; stolen by the killer who used it as his grisly trademark.

At first, King County police Lieutenant Jackson Beard thought he was dealing with a straightforward sex killing – a man with too much to drink, picks up pretty girl, is denied what he wants, uses violence, panics, kills, and dumps the body. It was a gruesome crime, but far removed from the kind committed by the most daunting criminal who plagues police forces – the serial killer. He is the most feared of all wanted men because there is no apparent logic, no method or pattern to his madness which could leave valuable clues for lawmen to follow up.

Wendy Coffield was a child prostitute runaway from a nearby town, who had been missing for three months when she was discovered by the boys fishing on 15 July 1982. Five weeks later a one-off sex crime turned into the beginning of the nightmare that has yet to end for the petrified residents of King County. For in a single day three more bodies of young women were found in the river at separate locations.

Over the following years the bodies of women aged between 15 and 36 were found all over King County, in neighbouring Northern Pierce County, and the remains of two were discovered in the state of Oregon, which borders Washington. Police believe that for once the killer deviated from his practice of preying on the small towns and kidnapped his victims to butcher them elsewhere. So far the largest single police operation in US history to capture one man has failed. It has cost in the region of £14 million, involved detectives from seven police forces and the FBI, and has drawn a huge blank. The deck, say police, is stacked hugely in the killer's favour.

Now in the Seattle phone book is a permanent listing for a government agency that did not exist before that bright sunny day in July 1982. It is a seven digit number for the Green River Task Force which waits night and day for new information which could lead to the capture of the killer. Fae Brooks, a spokeswoman for the group which has been formed especially to try to track down the psycopathic sex killer said: 'In terms of statistics, the guy doesn't stop until he is dead or until he's caught. In fact, if anything, it may be that he has gotten more clever over the years.'

Some of the problems the police faced were not in overcoming the ruthlessness or cunning of the killer, but of the attitude of the local population. Although petrified that a killer was stalking the Ivy League fields, mountains and ravines of the communities, police say the local populace developed an unhealthy, complacent attitude towards the murderer because so many of his victims had been involved at some stage of their lives with prostitution. One of the missing girls, nineteen-year-old Tracy Winston, a young prostitute, is now thought to have fallen victim to him in 1983. Her mother summed up the feelings of the grieving parents when she said that attention was being diverted away from catching the killer with the public demanding action against prostitution instead. 'Our kids are being penalized again', she said. 'It sounds silly, but how can you be penalized any more after you've been murdered? We admit freely and openly that our kids had problems but Tracy didn't deserve to die because she wasn't living what was perceived to be a perfect life. The issue was and is this maniac out there, not the lives that some of his victims were leading.'

Lieutenant Dan Nolan of King County Sheriff's Department is a patient man who has been in the police force all his life, and at fifty-two, looks more like a businessman than a policeman. He has worked on every case from traffic offences to first degree murder, and is regarded by his colleagues as a patient, thorough policeman who leaves no stone unturned in his quest for justice. He is second-in-command of the Green River Task Force whose lives have centred on catching this man over the years. He says: 'The man we're looking for is a shade of grey. He is very innocuous, fits right into the community. That is what makes him so very dangerous.'

To protect the investigation the police have revealed little about their suspect, apart from issuing a photofit and these scant details: he is thought to be middle-aged and an outdoors-type who knows the mountains, ravines and streams of the area like the back of his hand. He is remarkably strong, being able to carry the body of a fully grown woman for some distances. On a few occasions witnesses have glimpsed the victims with strange men shortly before they were discovered dead. From these sketchy sightings, police believe that the killer could drive a light-blue pick-up truck speckled with primer paint covering rust spots.

He is a sexual psychopath, his mind tormented perhaps, say experts, by some deep, dark secret from his childhood which induces the terrible anger he vents on his innocent victims. Police will not comment on how he kills his victims, although one psychologist who has worked with them to build up a picture of the death says that the killer probably favours strangulation so he is able to watch his victims suffer as he snuffs the life from them.

The Green River Killer is, above all, very, very clever. He has turned lush meadows and lonely woodlands within a 45 mile radius of Seattle into 'cluster dumps' for his victims. Bodies have been found by mushroom pickers, hunters and joggers, by boy scouts and apple pickers, by bottle scroungers and boys with fishing rods. In one case an amiable psychic said she was drawn straight to the skeleton of one victim after seeing visions of the dead girl over a seven day period. So far there have been 10,000 tips telephoned into the Green River Task Force centre, a handful of bogus confessions from sick glory seekers and 1,000 suspects quizzed – everyone from a devil worshipper to a police officer himself. So far, nothing. Even the faces of two unidentified bodies have been re-constructed by a film expert who worked on the feature film *Gorky Park*. In the film the faces of murder victims in Moscow are re-constituted to help authorities discover their identities. The practice was copied on the two dead women, but it has neither solved their identities nor the identity of the killer.

Lieutenant Nolan, who has been second in command of the hunt for the killer since 1984 says that police officers on the team have learned to live with the disappointment that they have not yet managed to capture the killer. 'The feeling was certainly that we would solve it within a year. When that didn't happen I think we were all frustrated and certainly pretty disappointed. We kind of hit the wall in January 1985. A lot of people started pointing inwardly and saying: "Am I doing my job well enough? Is it possible to solve?" We got clinical psychologists to come out and talk to us about the stress we were going through. We got to a point where we agreed that this was the most difficult investigation that we had ever been involved with and by God, it certainly was worth it and we were going to stay with it until it was solved.'

There is a grudging respect within the Task Force that their quarry is a man who picks his victims well, leaving his hunters with little in the way of witnesses or clues. Unless the police are holding back, apart from the *modus operandi* of their deaths, there is little the killer leaves behind to point them in the right direction. Nolan went on: 'Because he conceals the bodies, because he doesn't want them found quickly, he is clever. Very, very clever. It makes determining death more difficult, leaves no clues.'

The killer has now not struck for three years. Why? Nolan speculates: 'The possibility exists that he's in jail, that he's dead, that he has moved out of the area or out of the country – or that he has quit killing. That is probably the least likely – someone who would commit this number of killings isn't suddenly likely to find his appetite sated.' He added: 'I would love to capture him, to get him to sit down and tell me just why he did this, what drove him. I don't have any idea what this guy's going to tell me, what his secret is. He is still out there, a man with such terrible secrets. . . .'

The Man in the Iron Mask

The great novelist Alexander Dumas immortalized him in his novel of the same name – the story of the wretch kept imprisoned in a mask of iron, his identity shielded from the world, the secret of his crime lodged only with the King and perhaps a few of his trusted advisers. He wore the mask for thirty years, ate with it on, slept with it on. Even at his death the flanged contraption stayed on his face. Who was he? What was the secret of his crime? It is a mystery that has endured to this day with many theories put forward but few concrete answers.

It was on the personal command of the Sun King, Louis XIV, ruler of France, builder of the great Palace of Versailles, that the identity of the man in the iron mask was kept secret – not only from his subjects, but from his court and the jailors. To that end, for three decades, he lived in solitary confinement in different prisons, ending his days in France's most infamous jail, the Bastille. In 1703 when he died, the furniture in his cell was burned, the whitewash on the walls was re-painted to erase any pathetic epitaph to the world and the metalwork of his mask was melted down. Those who had kept his identity secret in life were determined that he should remain anonymous even when he was dead.

The rumours of the man in the iron mask abounded in France before the revolution. Louis was a deity, a divine ruler, whose harsh laws sentenced bread stealers to years of servitude aboard the galleys and death for stealing apples from the royal orchards. Even in an illiterate society as France was at that time, it was no wonder that word of the strange prisoner in the bowels of the Bastille spread across the land. What was he guilty of that spared his life – but condemned him to this living death, trapped in a mask of iron? No correspondence exists between prison officials and court functionaries, but the people had their own fantastic theories. One was that he was Louis XIV's twin brother, who was shut away on the orders of the vain glorious emperor in order to preserve the throne and its privileges for himself. Another theory suggested that he was the illegitimate child of a farm girl, born after a dalliance with the King, and that his resemblance was so close to that of his father that he was imprisoned forever.

Imprisoned for a lifetime.

It was not until fifty years after his death that historians began to probe into the identity of this strange man, and to discover what his crime had been. In 1753, exactly fifty years after he died in the Bastille, a journal kept by one Etienne du Jonca surfaced in Paris. Du Jonca was a lieutenant of the King; literate, educated – and curious. He recorded that in 1698, when the unfortunate man had already spent nearly thirty years behind bars, he was sent to the prison as the King's emissary. He recorded the following: 'Thursday 18 September at 3.00 o'clock, Monsieur de Saint-Mars, Governor of the Château of the Bastille, made his appearance, coming from the command of the Iles-Sainte-Marguerite Pignerol with a prisoner, whom he always caused to be masked, whose name is not mentioned.'

Five days after recording his arrival at the Bastille, du Jonca wrote of the man's death, saying that his removal from the cell and the subsequent burning of his furniture and clothes was carried out with 'great haste'. The King's Lieutenant also noted that the prisoner wore a mask of black velvet and not of iron when he saw him laid out for burial in an unmarked grave. (Whether this was done as a belated attempt at decency by the authorities or not – saving him from burial in the infernal mask – we shall never know.) Etienne du Jonca then testified that the man was buried under the false name of Marchioly. No prison official was allowed to gaze at the face beneath the mask as the corpse was transported from the Bastille under cover of darkness to an unmarked grave somewhere in the vicinity of the city. It is not even known whether or not he received a Christian burial, but it seems likely, for du Jonca also noted that the prisoner received one privilege not usually afforded to inmates of the Bastille – the right to a Bible and Christian worship.

At Villeneuve, in the Bourbonnais region of France, more clues surfaced about how closely guarded the secret of the man's identity was. Peasants there spoke of how, on his journey with the masked prisoner, the governor stopped with his charge at his own château for a meal. Peasants who glanced through the window saw how de Saint-Mars sat opposite his prisoner with two loaded pistols next to his plate, ready to discharge them if the captive made one attempt to reveal his identity to the domestic servants in the château.

Up until the French Revolution in 1789, it was presumed that only de Saint-Mars and the King knew the identity of the prisoner. It was certainly not passed on within the House of Bourbon for neither of Louis' successors knew who he was – and the last ruler of France, Louis XVI, began a frantic search for it at the request of his wife, Marie Antoinette.

When the French Revolution overturned Europe's established order in a tidal wave of change, numerous government agencies were ransacked by rising politicians such as Robespierre. Often the aim was to find information valuable for their own ends; however papers found in the Minister of War's office in Paris shed intriguing light on the secret of France's most celebrated captive. It transpired that for years de Saint-Mars had corresponded with a man named Louvois, a functionary of some kind in the prison service. In July 1669, Louvois wrote to de Saint-Mars: 'The King has commanded that I am to have the man named Eustache Dauger sent to Pignerol. It is of the utmost importance to his service that he should be most securely guarded and that he should in no way give information about himself nor send letters to anyone at all. You will yourself, once a day, have to take enough food for the day to this wretch and you must on no account listen for any reason at all to what he may want to say to you, always threatening to kill him if he opens his mouth to speak of anything but his necessities.' Then another letter, from the King himself, was also unearthed in the War Minister's archives, written to de Saint-Mars, which said: 'I am sending to my citadel of Pignerol, in the charge of Captain de Vauroy, sergeant major of my city and citadel of Dunkirk, the man named Eustache Dauger. You are to hold him in good and safe custody; prevent him from communicating with anyone at all, by word of mouth or writ of hand. So be it.'

Up until the discovery of these letters it was widely believed that the false name he was buried under, Marchioly, was a bastardization of Mattioli, an envoy of the Duke of Mantua who had once incurred the King's wrath. Mattioli did indeed end up in penal servitude in Pignerol, but he and the man in the iron mask were two separate people.

Nineteenth century research into Eustache Dauger proved this: he was one of six brothers, four of whom fell in battle. He came from the northern French fishing port of Dunkirk and was believed at one time to have been a lieutenant in the elite King's Guards – a feat made possible by virtue of his brother's elevation to the nobility.

With his brother circulating in court circles, and himself guarding the heart of the realm, Eustache came close to the wicked Madame de Montespan, the King's mistress and a dabbler in black magic. Those close to the royal circle knew that de Montespan was strong medicine for the King, and that he tolerated her heretical indulgences because he was fascinated by her. It is possible, therefore, that Eustache Dauger became entranced by her, went to a black mass, and was discovered by the King. He could not have him spreading the word that the King's concubine indulged in devil worship. Perhaps that was the reason for the years in jail. Perhaps he was merely jealous, paranoid that a mere soldier was set to steal his sweetheart from him. But why not have him executed? Louis was, after all, a monarch with absolute power.

To this day the secret of the man in the iron mask remains as steadfast as the forged metal which kept his face from the world for over thirty years.

Chapter Two

STATE SECRETS

Spies and spymasters play their never-ending games behind a cloak of secrecy that shields a *mélange* of dirty tricks, blackmail and murder. Read about the spectacular kidnapping of top Nazi Adolf Eichmann by the Israeli secret service; the nightclub dancer whose fatal charms led her into the beds of top military men and ultimately to face a firing squad; and the Rosenbergs, the couple whose twisted allegiance to Moscow made them sell their nation's greatest secret.

Haiti's Voodoo Police

Haiti is one of the poorest countries in the world. Its six million inhabitants exist on an income per head of less than £200 each year. Infants have a one in fifty chance of reaching their first birthday. What little industry there is centres on a few paltry millions made from rum, molasses and tourism. The Haitian people are a bright, sparkling French and Creole speaking nation who struggle in the grip of two terrible forces that have ravaged their land. One is corruption – the other is voodoo.

Haiti is under the spell of voodoo. A popular saying goes that the largely Catholic population worships voodoo gods six days a week – and on Sunday praises Jesus Christ. Haiti's infamous dictator Francois 'Papa Doc' Duvalier realized the sway that voodoo held over his poor blighted land and harnessed it with a vengeance. He created an elite security force which protected him, allowing him to rule over the Caribbean republic like a feudal king. This secret service were the Tonton Macoutes – Haiti's voodoo police. Like the the Gestapo and the KGB, they ruled by fear and kept Papa Doc in riches and power while the wretched masses suffered. The Tonton Macoutes were his praetorian guard, his secret police, his death squads. They controlled every facet of life in Haiti and left behind them a legacy of 40,000 corpses when Papa Doc died in 1971. After him came fifteen years more rule by Jean-Claude 'Baby Doc' Duvalier who, in the fine tradition of despotic dictatorships declared himself President for Life until he had to flee for his life in 1986. Thus ended the brutal reign of the infamous Tonton Macoutes who had probably killed another 20,000 people under the presidency of Baby Doc. What was the secret of their power?

Voodoo is one of the darkest, oldest religions in the world. Even as the people of Haiti starve and succumb to disease, the grip of the religion holds them like a vice. In Port-au-Prince, the capital, there are motor cars and hotels with marble entrances, staffed with polite but restrained natives. But in the hills, when the sun goes down, those same people will offer up blood sacrifices, walk on hot coals and become possessed by demons in their enslavement to black magic.

Voodoo has been in the blood of the Haitian people ever since the late seventeenth century when the French populated their former colony with slaves from west Africa. The religion dwindled through the years in Africa,

Two Tonton members ride past a ceremonial parade.

but remained a potent force on the island. It is a religion which worships the dark side of man's soul, involving summoning up the dead, offering animals for sacrifice and entering into trance-like states.

Papa Doc Duvalier was an evil, corrupt man who knew that harnessing the beliefs and superstitions of the population would, by association, give him great power over them. He came to office in 1957, after Haiti had endured forty years of military rule – first an occupation by the United States and then a military junta. In 1957 Papa Doc took the reins of power and embarked on his voodoo dynasty.

When he was a medical doctor in 1944, plotting his rise to power, he made a study of voodooism because he knew it would make him popular among the superstitious, illiterate peasants. He wrote a book called *The Gradual Evolution of Voodoo* in which he praised the black art as if it were as innocent as a Hans Christian Andersen folk story. He wrote: 'Every country has its own folklore. It is part of its patrimony. It is so in England, Japan and Central Europe.' He then went on to extol the virtues of voodoo as a natural and integral part of the Haitian character. When he became president he wore

Paris suits and English shoes – but the beating of the voodoo drums was never very far from his heart.

Duvalier was a tyrant interested primarily with making life as comfortable and rich for himself as he could, at the expense of the wretched country he ruled over. He promised social reform, education and prosperity. He delivered torture, fear and an iron-fisted rule which ended in death for thousands of his opponents.

When he ruled Haiti, the population lived in fear of his dreaded Tonton Macoutes – the word literally means bogeymen in the Creole dialect. The Tontons were licensed torturers, murderers and robbers. To guarantee the safety of the despot, they took what they wanted from the cringing population, who believed the Tontons were the servants of Baron Samedei – the spirit of death. Many Haitians believed that Papa Doc was the reincarnation of Baron Samedei on Earth.

Papa Doc changed the colours of the Haitian flag to red and black – the colours of secret voodoo societies – and unleashed the Tontons on their bloody mission. The secret of their power lay in the fear they generated among Haiti's inhabitants. No one was immune from their reach because the president himself had sanctioned their crusade. And the power of the voodoo was with them. In that first year alone, an ex-Tonton later said as many as 600 people died, their throats slit, or their heads bashed in with rocks in remote regions of the island. The world knew little of this wholesale terror for many years – to outsiders Papa Doc retained the image of a philanthropic doctor intent on raising Haiti's poor living standards. To the frightened population he was the voodoo master who, at night, was said to store the bodies of the Tontons in his palace cellar, performing black magic rites upon them until they became Zombies – the living dead. In 1967 when Elizabeth Taylor and Richard Burton starred with Alec Guinness in the screen version of Graham Greene's novel *The Comedians* – a scathing book about life under Duvalier in Haiti – the President was moved to voodoo. Ex-aides reported that he had effigies made of the stars – and stuck them with pins!

The Tontons hid behind the president's power. Armed, hiding behind sinister sunglasses, they displayed none of the sophistication of a secret intelligence service – they were merely the secret police force of a ruthless dictator. They ravaged the land, bartering chickens, flour, jewellery in exchange for lives. In Haitian legend the bogeyman traditionally visited households at Christmas and took naughty children away in his knapsack, never to be seen again. In reality, the Tonton Macoutes carried away thousands of people in their bloody rampage.

While the bogeymen fleeced their countrymen, Papa Doc fleeced the country – creaming off millions in foreign aid to satisfy his lust for fast cars, excellent wines, lavish furnishings. In eccentric gestures he often rode through the presidential gates and threw money from his Mercedes car to the pathetically poor people.

Duvalier went to extremes in his belief in the power of voodoo. He once sent a Tonton Macoute agent to President Kennedy's grave in Arlington Cemetery in Virginia, the United States' most hallowed graveyard for statesmen and warrior sons, to collect a pinch of earth, a withered flower and a vial of air. Papa Doc wanted them for a voodoo rite to imprison President Kennedy's soul and thus control US foreign policy in the area. It is estimated that he built up a personal fortune of some 500 million US dollars, stored safely in Swiss bank vaults.

Duvalier's secret army, dressed in their blue shirts and red scarves, kept the terrified population docile. Through the voodoo priests in the villages, the bogeymen made sure that dues were paid. It was, as one American correspondent observed in 1971, after Papa Doc's death, 'terror by consent'.

After his father's death, Baby Doc Duvalier ascended to the presidency of the embattled republic. Like father, like son, he also exploited and used the terror of the Tonton Macoutes – and if anything he was more ruthless and more greedy than his father.

By the time his father died, the secret of the Tontons was out in the west. Aid from the United States was cut and the Tontons had their name changed to the Volunteers for National Security. It was a name only; they continued with their old ways, murdering, torturing, stealing.

The end came for the tyrant Baby Doc and his servants, the Tontons, in 1986. The President for Life fled for his life after pressure from the United States and internal dissent threatened to engulf him. His departure wreaked a terrible revenge on the Tonton Macoutes whose spell was broken; dozens were dragged out of their homes and butchered with the very machetes which they had wielded against so many helpless victims.

Haiti is still desperately poor and its people the pawns in a never-ending power struggle between politicians and the military. There were two coups in the country this year alone. Newsmen who flooded into the country were shown the graves of the Tontons' victims, Haiti's own killing fields where the unfortunates who couldn't meet their robbing demands or who were deemed undesirables by the Duvaliers, were dumped. The spectre of the bogeyman is lifted – but the voodoo worshippers of Haiti wonder how long the respite will last before another Baron Samedei and his Tontons visit them.

The Eichmann Affair

After the KGB, the CIA and MI5, one agency stands out as the most capable, the most cunning, the most ruthless of the smaller intelligence networks which exist in the world. It is the Mossad, an organization dedicated to the preservation of Israel. In a hostile world, its operatives and agents are more than employees – they are disciples of the state of Israel and understand that the maxim of 'know thine enemy' applies more rigorously to them than to any superpower. The Mossad lives by the creed of a German-born Jewish scientist named Charles Proteus Steinmetz, a pioneering electrical engineer. He once wrote: 'There will come an àge of small and independent nations whose first line of defence will be knowledge.' That has become the motto of the Mossad and indeed it could be said to be the motto of the entire Israeli nation. By staying one step ahead of its enemies, Israel has survived and flourished as the spiritual home for the world's Jewish population.

But it was one spectacular act which earned the Mossad the admiration of global spymasters – a top secret operation concerned not with the security of Israel, but an act of revenge, of vengeance, of atonement for the years the Jewish people suffered during the Holocaust. For the Mossad traced, identified and kidnapped one of the most wanted Nazi war criminals. It was a brilliant coup and the forerunner of Israel's policy to this day – that no terrorist is safe, no criminal ever totally free.

Before the kidnapping of Adolf Eichmann in 1960, the Mossad had established itself as the main intelligence agency in the Zionist state. It was born out of the pre-independence days when Jewish guerrillas fought British colonial rule in Palestine. The Haganah, the underground army formed by the Jewish settlers in Palestine, spawned five intelligence branches during the struggle for independence. One of them was the Mossad – in Hebrew, the Institution for Intelligence and Special Assignments. The primary task of the agency, reformed and restructured after the war of independence by prime minister David Ben-Gurion, was to complete Israel's dirty and undesirable tasks, with discretion and success.

Isser Harel was the first chief of the Mossad and most, probably its best. Harel knew no fear, knew no boundaries in his mission to serve the state. He was known as 'Isser the Little' who emigrated from Latvia in 1930; more than any other individual he is credited for making the Mossad the organization it is today. Harel showed cunning and coolness from the first day he landed in Palestine, smuggling a handgun past the stringent British customs, which he had pledged to put to good use in the fight for a Jewish homeland.

After a dedicated war against the British forces, Harel was rewarded with the command of Shin Beth – Israel's second major intelligence service concerned with internal security. Less exciting than Mossad, Harel none the less put his heart and soul into the Shin Beth and within two years, in 1958, he assumed command of all Israeli intelligence operations.

Isser Harel's obsession with secrecy was something of a joke even within the ranks of the Mossad. A popular gag about him was: 'Did you hear about the time Isser jumped into a taxi and the driver asked him where he was going? Isser replied: "Its a secret."' But the apparent frivolity masked a devotion to their boss which was second to none. His height of four feet eight inches was no drawback; only to the public was he 'Isser the Little'. To the agents who knew and worked for him he was Isser the Giant. For a decade he was Israel's chief spymaster, ruling with an autocratic hand. He answered to no one, not even justifying the Mossad budget to the Israeli parliament. Such secrecy guaranteed him the intelligence coup of the century – and earned him a place in history.

Ricardo Klement was an ordinary man. He went to work at the same time each day, bought his wife flowers on her birthday and was nice to his children. In Buenos Aires there was nothing to distinguish him from the countless other foreigners who made up the population of this gracious city, often dubbed 'The Paris of South America.' He was of German extraction, but then so many were; like the British who shopped at the Harrods store in the city, they built their own community, embracing the best of the old world and the new. Only ... Ricardo Klement had a secret.

Years before, in Germany between 1933 and 1945, he was not Ricardo Klement. He was Adolf Eichmann and his job was mass murder.

Eichman enjoyed the patronage of the highest echelons of the Nazi party. He was a member of the feared SS, rising to the security section of the organization to control the 'Final Solution' – Hitler's euphemism for the extermination of the Jews. Eichmann was the planner. While dregs of humanity may have pulled the triggers and herded the unfortunates into the chambers, Eichmann was the controller – the man who lent intellectual credibility to the monstrous master plan. Six million people died as a result of his planning – the biggest mass murderer in history. What shocked the world was that he had escaped justice at the end of the war.

In 1957 a blind Jew living in a suburb of Buenos Aires heard from his daughter that she was being courted by a man who called himself Nicholas Eichmann. Something triggered itself in the old man's mind; perhaps that this could be the son of the infamous Adolf. He contacted a friend in the German police department – in turn he was put in touch with Fritz Bauer, the public prosecutor of the German province of Hesse. It was Bauer who subsequently delivered to Isser Harel in Tel Aviv the dossier on one of the top ten war criminals still at large. It led to an extraordinary meeting between Harel and David Ben-Gurion. 'I would like permission to bring Eichmann back to Israel,' said Harel.

'Do it,' replied the premier. He had sanctioned the boldest intelligence mission in peacetime of the twentieth century.

Not only was the mission unprecedented in its scope, but the implications of both its successful – or failed – execution were enormous. Harel was not asking for the extradition of Eichmann, trusting to the benevolence or otherwise of the Argentine government. He had known too long that South America was the 'rat run' for fugitive Nazis fleeting from the ruins of World War Two. Harel planned to kidnap Eichmann – a mission so secret that one breath of it would have spelled its end and disgraced Israel in the eyes of the world. No matter that they were after a war criminal – Harel knew that the worst crime in diplomatic and political eyes was the one of being caught.

He assembled a hand-picked team of volunteers within the Mossad ranks and in early 1958 an agent was sent to Buenos Aires on a reconnaissance mission. He checked out the address that the old Jew had relayed to them – 4621 Chacabuco Street, in Olivos, a Buenos Aires suburb. Nothing. The family of Klement no longer lived there, the trail went cold. All the agent managed to gather was that a man whose physical traits resembled those of their quarry used to reside there, but his name was Klement. At the time, that meant nothing to Israeli intelligence.

It was not until 1959, after a Mossad agent paid a discreet visit to the elderly Jewish man, Lothar Hermann, that a detailed dossier was built up on the man they thought was Eichmann. Lother recalled, with the precise attention to detail that blind people have, the speech of his suspect and the physical attributes as they were told to him by his daughter. He also recalled one time when young Nicholas Eichmann had stood in his house and boasted about his father's war service.

A small team of crack Israeli agents, armed with the information supplied by Hermann, stayed on in Buenos Aires. But the budget of the Mossad was not then – and is not now – large enough to expend large amounts of cash without the likelihood of firm results. Harel was on the brink of cancelling the whole operation when in December 1959 an agent picked up a lead. After trailing Nicholas Eichmann from a motor cycle repair shop to a suburb in the

San Fernando district of the city, they were sure they had their quarry. But how sure? The Mossad team had the words of a blind lawyer and a picture from seventeen years ago from SS files. They staked out the suspect house in Garibaldi Street.

The residence was photographed secretly from every angle. More agents were sent in from Israel. The balding bespectacled man did not know he was subject to the kind of scrutiny that once was the domain of the organization he belonged to. But was it him?

The positive proof came on 21 March 1960 when Ricardo Klement got off the bus near his home and walked towards his front door clutching a large bouquet of flowers. From the house came the sound of laughter, the start of a party. A woman greeted him warmly at the door.

One of the Mossad agents scrutinizing the shabby house looked in his dossier and discovered that 21 March was the silver wedding anniversary of SS Colonel Herr Adolf Eichmann. They had found the butcher's lair.

After that events moved rapidly. A team of full-time agents was established in Buenos Aires under the on-the-spot command of Isser Harel. He said he felt had had to take full and personal charge of the operation.

The plan was, in effect, like all the best plans – simple. A travel agency was setup in a European city – still a secret to this day – to process the travel documents and permits for the Mossad team to travel to Argentina. The group's overriding concern was not to be publicly seen to be violating the sovereignty of a friendly nation. There was no other way, however, than a covert mission. Argentina had long given sanctuary to the Nazi war criminals and an official approach, while it might have met with courtesy and public promises of action, would have led to the fugitive escaping into a neighbouring country, or even further abroad. Isser Harel, with the backing of Ben-Gurion, was not prepared to let that happen.

In Buenos Aires, 'safe' houses were rented all over the city. Agents processed by the 'laundry' travel agency flew in from various European cities – no two the same. On 11 May it was decided to snatch Adolf Eichmann.

There were tense moments outside the house on Garibaldi Street that night. Failure meant disgrace in the eyes of the world. Every agent, positioned in their safe houses and outside the home of Eichmann, knew that if the plan was wrong they could count only on their own resources to get clear – and there would be no welcoming committee back home.

Three buses which Eichmann usually caught coming home pulled up. All the passengers disembarked but Eichmann was not among them. On that cold night the Mossad agents prayed that he had not been tipped off and fled as so many other Nazis had.

At 8.00pm another bus arrived and Ricardo Klement, in reality Nazi

Adolf Eichmann, stepped off. The secret mission of the decade was on.

Eichmann wandered, with the same nonchalance that he usually displayed, to the door of his home. He passed a car that appeared to have broken down with two men studying the engine. He did not know that a third man was lying on the floor of the vehicle or that the car parked on the opposite side of the road was positioned to shine its lights directly in front of the parked vehicle he was walking towards. When he got near it he was sandwiched between a wall of light that temporarily blinded him. The man on the back seat of the car jumped out and, with the aid of the accomplices studying the engine compartment, bundled Eichmann into the back seat. With a pistol to his head they muttered: 'Make a sound and you are dead.'

An hour later and Eichmann was in one of the safe houses which the agents had rented. Shackled to a bed, Ricardo Klement was stripped of the identity which had shielded him from justice for fifteen years. The agents checked under his armpit for his SS number, but found only a scar – a crude removal had been attempted. But there was no pretence any longer. The bald man who had devised the timetable for the final solution stood in the pyjamas that the Mossad had bought for him and said: 'Ich bin Adolf Eichmann' – I am Adolf Eichmann.

After the enormity of their capture many of the Mossad agents were overcome with emotion. They had all lost loved ones in the Holocaust which Eichmann had kept running as a smoothly oiled train. Many said afterwards that they expected a monster – what they got was a faceless, balding bureaucrat who recited to them in perfect Hebrew the most holy of Jewish prayers.

Eichmann was kept in the safe house for over a week while phase two of the operation was organized – how to get him out of Argentina.

Harel played a hunch during this period. He thought that the family of Eichmann would go through the usual procedures of checking up where Ricardo Klement had got to – the hospitals, jails, private clinics. But he suspected they would not raise a worldwide hue and cry for a man wanted for some of history's most heinous crimes. And they were right – the secret was safe. Neither did the family set on the tail of the Israeli agents any Nazis who lived in sanctuary in Buenos Aires to pursue the Israelis.

However, soon the Nazi underground whisper was out that something unpleasant could have befallen 'Comrade Eichmann.' That was bad news for Israel and the civilized world too because Harel thought that Dr Josef Mengele, the bestial doctor who carried out grotesque experiments on inmates at the Auschwitz concentration camp was one of those who got away because of the whispers.

But getting Eichmann out of Argentina was the most serious obstacle.

Finally Isser Harel risked all on a simple ploy. He drugged Eichmann, dressed him and his agents in the uniform of El Al, the official airline of Israel, and arranged for a jet to be at Buenos Aires airport. He drove through with the drugged air-crewman, explained that he had sampled too much Agentine hospitality the night before, and asked permission to board the aircraft. 'He's not flying in that state, is he?' asked a customs guard. 'Oh no, we're only the reserve crew,' said Harel. They were through.

Back in Tel Aviv twenty-four hours later Isser the Little walked into David Ben-Gurion's office and said: 'I have brought a little present for you.'

The following day Ben-Gurion made the most moving speech he has ever made to the Israeli parlament, the Knesset:

'I have to announce that a short time ago one of the greatest of Nazi criminals was found by the Israeli secret service. Adolf Eichmann, who was responsible, together with the Nazi leaders, for what they called "The Final Solution of the Jewish Problem" – that is the extermination of six million Jews of Europe.

'Adolf Eichmann is already under arrest in Israel and he will shortly be brought to trial in Israel.'

The rest is history; Adolf Eichmann, who praised his captors from the dock, was found guilty of war crimes and sentenced to death. He was hanged.

The Taking of a Terrorist

The Western world has long groaned at the news of terrorists and their innocent victims for two reasons: first, that the victims are held hostage or killed for beliefs that are alien to them and second, that we seem powerless to do anything about the terrorists themselves. We have all endured the heartbreaking scenes from airports – flashed on to prime-time news reports – as a bundle that was once a human being is pushed from the doorway of a plane to land on the tarmac like excess baggage. In recent years terrorists have dramatically escalated their activities in the air and to a lesser extent at sea. In 1985, a TWA flight from Athens was hijacked shortly after take-off and US Navy diver Robert Stethem was murdered. In October of the same year the *Achille Lauro* ship was hijacked by Arab fanatics and a wheelchair bound US citizen, Leon Klinghoffer, was murdered. In December 1985 a wanton attack at Rome airport killed fifteen people – the massacre sanctioned by terror 'Godfather' Abu Nidal, who was sentenced in absentia by an Italian court to life imprisonment. On the same day Arab fanatics opened up with machine guns and hand grenades at Vienna Airport, killing three and wounding forty-one. The following April a bomb exploded on board a TWA jet as it approached Athens airport. Four US citizens died, and the suspect, a Lebanese woman thought to belong to a Palestinian terror group, escaped. On 5 April 1986 a bomb exploded in a discotheque in West Berlin, killing two US servicemen and wounding 200, including seventy Americans. In September of the same year, in an aborted hijacking in Pakistan, twenty people, were murdered. People groaned uncomfortably in the West – but what was to be done?

No one was more concerned than President Ronald Reagan, a man who put his own personal stamp on the presidency of the United States more than any postwar chief executive since John F. Kennedy. The Reagan years ushered in a new pride in the United States, a new patriotism and belief in the American way. But all that had happened on the international scene pointed to the fact that his citizens – and the citizens of the other 'free' world countries – were easy game for terrorists around the globe. The United States could not stoop to the level of the killers. What could be done? In January 1986 President Reagan signed an order which gave the mightiest nation in the world the right to strike back against the butchers – legally. In doing so he sanctioned one of Western intelligence's most secret operations since the end of the Cold War; a £10 million high-tech kidnapping whose message to terrorists everywhere rings loud and clear: there is no sanctuary anywhere. Reagan put into motion a mission so daring in its concept that it could almost have been penned for the pages of a *Boys' Own* annual. EXCEPT . . . it is true.

Fawaz Younis stood on the tarmac of Beirut airport, clad in a bullet-proof vest and ringed by five murderous looking accomplices who clutched Soviet-made AK 47 assault rifles and, incongruously, Uzi sub-machine guns – the arms of the state of Israel. Younis had just emerged from the cabin of a Royal Jordanian jet where he had overseen fifty-three hours of sheer brutality. The eight Jordanian guards, on his orders, had been tied and beaten senseless, the passengers terrorized in an airborne ordeal which at one time seemed doomed to end in bloodshed and death. However, the terrorists then decided on a course of action that few could have predicted. They released those held prisoner on board the plane and called a press conference. At the end of a rambling speech delivered to waiting cameramen and reporters, the fanatical gunmen on Younis' orders broke the silence of the June morning with the staccato thump of bullets from their weapons into the plane, setting off explosives which destroyed it completely. Then they vanished into the labyrinth of terrorist hideouts in Beirut.

Younis had emerged in the bloody battle-ground of the middle east as a power-player in lethal games. He had access to the top-level leaders of various Shiite militiamen and had been involved in several terror operations before the hijacking of the Royal Jordanian aircraft. He was one of the terrorists on the hijacked TWA flight which resulted in the death of US Navy diver Robert Stethem. More importantly, to US intelligence, he was 'visible', walking openly around Beirut and boasting of his evil trade. In 1986 it was decided to capture him and bring him to trial in the United States.

The mission to seize Younis was spawned at a top-secret meeting hosted by President Reagan in January 1986. Frustrated at the inability of the world's democracies to hit back at terrorism, the President signed a classified intelligence document authorizing the CIA to identify terrorists who had committed crimes abroad and to help bring them to trial in the USA. It gave the authority for Operation Goldenrod to be put into action.

Goldenrod's aim was to capture Younis after he had been 'targeted' by US intelligence agents in Beirut. His crimes were not as heinous as those of the killer aboard TWA Flight 847, or of the Rome or Vienna murderers, but he had broken international law by leading a hi-jack. More importantly, he had not gone to ground. There was a further meeting with the President in October 1986 in which the final sanction was given to capture Younis.

The operation was to be a tri-partisan affair between the CIA, the DEA and the FBI, with the latter's executive assistant director Oliver Revell heading the effort. He told the team: 'This is going to be one of the most important counter-terrorism operations ever staged by the US government.' But the problems facing the team were immense. Reagan did not want the United States branded with piracy over a kidnapping. Nor did he want to run the risk of losing Younis on the long route back home to the United States; this one, he decreed, was for the US alone. It meant that somehow Younis would have to be lured on to a ship or an aeroplane and then taken at all speed, and without stopping, to the United States.

Fortunately for the planners, a bit of good fortune came their way early on with the news that an informer had been recruited by DEA officials in Cyprus. There, on the island that has become a staging post for drug runners and small-time arms dealers, was a disillusioned Lebanese man called Jamal Hamdan. Hamdan used to live in Beirut and was once the driver and right-hand man for a guerrilla leader, with whom he shared an apartment for six months. That man was called Fawaz Younis.

Hamdan agreed to sell information on drug peddlers and other crooks whenever he received knowledge at his home in Larnaca. But Goldenrod's architects saw in him someone far more valuable than a low-level 'grass' on hashish movements. They saw him as the bait to trap Younis. By getting Hamdan to agree to re-establish his friendship with Younis, they set in motion the first steps to getting Younis on to US soil.

The first link was made in March 1987 when Hamdan called Younis from his apartment. They talked about old times, the weather, Younis' two children. It was the first of over sixty calls which led to Hamdan inviting the terrorist to his apartment in July. The bearded terrorist did not know that when he arrived a team of electronic 'spooks' from the three US agencies involved had been there before him, turning the apartment into a giant listening device. Bugs bristled in the bathroom, kitchen, bedroom, even in the toilet. The United States was determined that if Fawaz Younis was going to be tried, he would damn himself with his own evidence.

The listening devices paid off. Younis not only boasted of his role in the Royal Jordanian skyjacking but also his part in the TWA one in which a US Navy diver died. The listeners recording his boasts realized that Younis would be valuable for information about guerrilla factions in Beirut when he let it slip that he had received orders for the hijacking from none other than Nabih Berry, the head of the Amal militia. One of the extracts which the FBI released has Younis talking about the June 1985 hijacking which ended with the plane being destroyed. He said: 'I got inside and I locked the plane's captain in the cockpit. The people were on the floor, their hands on their heads. Everyone, no exceptions. I got a stewardess and asked her about the security men. There were eight. I took their neckties and tied their hands behind their backs. We started beating them. We took four machine guns and eight pistols from them. We kept them tied up for forty-eight hours. We stayed fifty-three hours flying.'

There was a second visit to Hamdan in August, during which the 'friends' went on a five-day bar crawl around the island's clubs. At this meeting Younis had complained that he was short of money. Hamdan, supplied from a special slush-fund set up for the operation, handed Younis US $4000. The news of his cash problems was good for the secret agents. They knew they could probably capitalize on that to their advantage. When Younis visited

Cyprus for a second time that month, the lure of earning big money, tax free, was put in front of him. Hamdan said that a drug dealing friend known as Joseph was willing to pay big money for someone to act as a courier for his illegal merchandise. Would Younis be interested? He said he would.

Once Younis agreed that he would consider any option – as his second-hand car dealing business was bankrupt and he had little money from taxi-driving in Beirut – Goldenrod's controllers put in phase two of their plan; luring him off Cyprus soil and getting him to the United States as fast as possible. There was no way President Reagan would tolerate having Younis' feet touch any soil other than American. The hijackers of the *Achille Lauro*, who murdered a wheel-chair bound American citizen, were forced down in their Tunisian-bound jet in Italy where the authorities insisted on trying them there. Reagan said only US justice was to try Younis – and that was final.

Commander Philip Voss is one of the most experienced pilots in the US forces. He has clocked up over 3,000 flying hours alone on the S-3 Lockheed Viking aircraft, one of less than twenty fliers in the world with as much experience. He was in charge of a squadron of the anti-submarine aircraft aboard the USS Saratoga, an aircraft carrier, when on 27 August 1987, he received a top-level security cleared call from Washington to say he would be involved in a highly secret mission requiring him to fly a great distance. He was told that it would be from somewhere in the Mediterranean to somewhere in the United States. He was told to plan the logistics of re-fuelling and routing, but not to breathe a word about what was being planned. When he drew up a plan he was told to wait and remain silent.

On 7 September FBI officials, together with Pentagon chiefs, decided on the final stages of the plan and the next day it was presented to Attorney General Edwin Meese. He signed it. Goldenrod was on and running.

On 10 September Younis returned to Cyprus for his assignment with the mystery drug runner Joseph. To keep up the appearance of a free-spending pal, more cash was forwarded from the agencies' slush fund for Hamdan to entertain his friend. As the duo lifted their glasses in 'cheers' in a Larnaca nightclub, the ink was just drying on an arrest warrant that had been signed for Fawaz Younis. Hamdan told him that they were to meet with Joseph on the boat he used to transport his merchandise and so the pair stayed the night of 12 September at the Sheraton Hotel in Limassol. The following morning Hamdan's 'brother' – a CIA man – ferried them from the shore to an eighty foot yacht which looked as if it might have a wealthy owner. The trip took ninety minutes, so the yacht was well out into international waters.

Younis dressed as if he were headed for a deck party. He wore beige shorts, a green shirt and sandals, expensive gold rings, necklace and watch. As Hamdan had warned him he would be, he was searched, as Joseph insisted on security aboard his vessel. Then he was given a cool beer and led to the stern where he could talk with Joseph about the job. When he reached the back of the boat, two men nodded at each other in unison. Then acting together they kicked his legs, sending him plummeting to the wooden deck. He hit it so hard that he instantly broke both his wrists. As his hands were bound, FBI special Dimitry Droujinski told him in Arabic he was under arrest by the government of the United States of America and would be sent there for trial. He said nothing, but his look of stunned disbelief spoke volumes.

Within an hour the yacht had met up with the USS *Butte*, a navy ammunition ship which took charge of the wounded Younis and set sail for the Balearic islands to meet up with the USS *Saratoga* and the S-3 plane which would take Younis to the United States.

It took four days to reach the aircraft carrier, during which time Younis was quizzed and admitted his part in the hijackings. Then on 17 September he was strapped into the S-3 plane and catapulted off the deck of the carrier at a speed of 135 miles per hour. The plane then linked up with a circling tanker which replaced the fuel load burned during take-off. 'It's a goer' signalled Voss to the ship and headed his plane on the course for home.

Halfway across the Atlantic he hooked up with the second tanker aircraft for re-fuelling. After that he had just one more hurdle – the civilian air traffic controllers at Andrews Air Force Base in Maryland who had not been told about the operation because the military feared possible security leaks. After a thirteen hour ten minute flight – the longest solo flight in history accomplished from an aircraft carrier – Commander Voss was asked to identify himself before being given permission to land. Luckily officials monitoring the challenge interrupted and told the air traffic controllers: 'Stop him and you explain yourself to the President.' They let him through.

Fawaz Younis was surrounded by fifteen FBI limousines as he stepped from the aircraft in the pouring rain. His trip to meet Joseph had been a one-way ticket halfway across the world into captivity.

He now awaits trial in solitary confinement. A jubilant state department official said: 'We hope this new policy hits home to terrorists everywhere. You can run – but you can never hide. He will be the first of many.'

The Rosenbergs

The date was the 19 June, the year 1953. Old Sparky, the name given to the electric chair in Sing Sing prison, was being tested by Joseph Frankel, who lived near the infamous jail in Cairo, New York. 'Electrician' Joe, as he was known, was due to collect 300 dollars for his night's work – despatching a pale skinny man and his slightly plumper wife to their maker. In his time Joe had plunged the switch and sent the electricity surging through the bodies of countless mafia hitmen, rapists, robbers, nickel-and-dime killers. But tonight was different. Tonight Joe was making history as he threw the switch which would send Julius and Ethel Rosenberg into oblivion. They were spies who sold out their country to the communists at a time when the cold war was at its coldest – in fact the only enemy agents ever to be executed in the United States in peacetime.

Shortly before midnight Joe placed the electrodes on Julius Rosenberg's head, strapped the other electrodes to his chest and arms, and placed a leather hood over his face. Two minutes and forty-five seconds later, with smoke still in the air, he was pronounced dead. After a few minutes to clear the air, his wife was brought in and the ghastly scenario was repeated. After four minutes and thirty seconds she too was pronounced dead. The Rosenbergs, who had made treachery their trade, were no more – two of the Kremlin's most valuable agents, who buried themselves deeply into ordinary suburban life, paid the ultimate price for their actions. This is their story.

Outwardly the Rosenbergs were no different from thousands of other US citizens of Russian–Jewish descent whose forefathers had come to the land of the free to seek a better life. Both were raised in a close-knit community on the Lower East Side in New York, an ethnic melting pot which encompassed people of practically every race on earth. They were poor but, by all accounts, well loved. Ethel, whose maiden name was Greenglass, became a clerical worker after graduating from Seward Park High School. The bespectacled, austere looking Julius, who once nurtured a desire to become a Rabbi, opted instead for an engineering course at the City College of New York in Manhattan. It was at a dance one night that he met the woman who was to become his wife and partner in treachery.

The couple married in 1939, before the outbreak of World War Two, which would see the Germans marching over Europe. Until 1945 Julius was a civilian in the Army Signals Corps and earned fifty dollars a week for

Ethel and Julius Rosenberg.

inspecting electrical equipment. It was a easy job and one which didn't require him to see active service overseas. He lived with his wife in Greenwich Village during the war years and they had two sons, Michael and Robert. Always financially insecure, the Rosenbergs made do like thousands of others and managed to muddle through with the dream that one day things would be better. But they were different from the majority of other people who came to America to earn the mighty dollar and fulfil their dreams. For they were communists who believed that the international socialist doctrine preached from Moscow was the only creed worth adhering to. Julius had been a communist from his earliest days in college. He was clever enough to keep the fact quiet – then, as now, the most stridently anti-communist country was the United States. His covert membership of the US communist party cost him his job in 1945. He was fired when a routine FBI investigation of personnel proved his allegiance to Moscow. With a family to feed, he opened up his own business, Pitt Engine Products, in the same building as a synagogue in down town New York. The venture was plagued by bad cash-flow and poor management. However, Julius struggled on with it and did not have to worry about a knock on the door from the FBI because of his strongly held beliefs. But the knock did come eventually – and it was eventually to cost the doomed Ethel and Julius Rosenberg their lives.

For nondescript Julius Rosenberg, together with his wife and her brother, David Greenglass, sold the United States' most prized secret – the formula for the atomic bomb, to the Soviet Union. It was the most heinous of crimes against a state which had assumed the role of free-world protection.

David Greenglass was seized by the FBI on 15 June 1950 and questioned at length. Greenglass worked at the top-secret Los Alamos site in New Mexico during the war years making 'lenses' – the detonators for the atomic bomb. Everyone within the complex that produced the A-bombs which wiped out Hiroshima and Nagasaki were security-cleared in case of alien loyalties. Greenglass had slipped through the net.

From Los Alamos he stole detailed drawings of the atomic bomb, together with copious notes of how it worked, how it was assembled, what was required to make it. His D-I-Y atom bomb secrets were fed directly through Julius and Ethel to Moscow emissaries in the United States and back to the Kremlin. Greenglass was caught as part of a wide-reaching FBI probe and, to save his own skin, readily implicated the Rosenbergs.

It turned out that a pathetic little Swiss immigrant called Harry Gold, who was the US courier for another major spy, was the go-between for the Rosenbergs and Greenglass. He would meet Greenglass using a code procedure worked out by Rosenberg. At a secret rendezvous point Gold would hand Greenglass the top of a jelly packet with the words 'I come from Julius' written on it. This meant that the coast was still clear and that the Rosenbergs required more information to pass on to their Soviet spymasters.

The United States led the world in nuclear research and had overtaken the Nazis in the race for atomic supremacy. Selling the secrets of their technology was just about the worst crime that they could have committed – especially as it was discovered in the McCarthy Era when the senator of the same name embarked on his witch hunts to root out anything and everyone deemed to be left wing and un-American in their actions, deeds and thoughts.

Gold, who worked as a chemist in Philadelphia before he became embroiled in espionage, was also the courier for top spy Klaus Fuchs. Fuchs was born in Germany and became a communist in his teens. When Hitler came to power he fled to England where he became a citizen. He was part of the British mission given top-level clearance to witness research and tests on the bomb. He too used the services of Gold and confessed to spying in 1950, receiving a fourteen year prison term. To this day it is not known whether he worked independently of the Rosenbergs or with them.

Another person indicted with the Rosenbergs was Morton Sobell, once Julius Rosenberg's classmate at college, who passed on secrets to the couple about the latest radar technology he worked on for the US Navy.

The arrests came in 1950 – Julius first in July and his wife twenty-five days later. The FBI dossier on the Rosenbergs and the others ran to some 40,000 pages and chronicled the information which they had channeled to Moscow in the years 1940 to 1948. At their trial it was claimed that their acts of treason alone had given Russia the Atom bomb – they exploded their first in 1949 when American intelligence had reckoned that it would have taken them fifteen years at least to catch up in the nuclear race. Thanks to the Rosenberg's misty-eyed idealism, the Russian bear was armed, ready for the cold war and the build-up of ballistic missiles.

The fifteen day trial in 1951 was a sensation which riveted the world. Gold's testimony particularly damned the couple as he told of the secret rendezvous he kept with Greenglass. And Greenglass in turned showed no emotion as he poured out the details of the secrets which would send his own sister and brother-in-law to the electric chair. Although he passed the secrets of the bomb on to Julius, he said his sister was a willing co-conspirator who was glad to play her part in ending 'world fascism'. He said she often stayed up late at night and typed up the careful notes which would be passed on to their Soviet controllers.

Another star witness was Elizabeth Bentley, who testified for the government. A Columbia university graduate, she told how she was lured into the ranks of the communists through several disastrous love affairs with Soviet agents. Though without direct knowledge of the Rosenberg's activities, she nevertheless played a crucial role for the state in its conspiracy charges against the couple – testifying that all communists were harmful to the United States because their loyalty lay with Moscow alone.

The jury were convinced and returned guilty verdicts, confirming that the Rosenbergs, who said nothing at all at their trial other than that they were innocent, conspired to commit espionage against the United States in time of war. They were handed down the death penalty by Judge Irving Kaufman, who branded them 'despicable traitors' and, rightly or wrongly, said their actions had led to the Korean war in which 50,000 Americans were to lose their lives. He said Julius had been the 'prime mover' of 'this diabolical conspiracy' and Ethel 'a fully fledged partner'.

Morton Sobell got a thirty year sentence, of which he served sixteen. David Greenglass, who stole the secrets but did not pass them on to the Soviets directly, was treated remarkably leniently, receiving a fifteen year sentence. He is now out of jail and lives under a new name somewhere near New York. Despite twenty two appeals and stays of execution, Julius Rosenberg, thirty-five, and Ethel, thirty-seven, had to die for an administration that demanded blood for the betrayal of its mightiest secrets.

After the switch was thrown that night and the Rosenberg children were adopted by another couple, the doubts and inquests on their guilt or innocence were raised around the world. In Cuba twenty-five years on the Castro regime even issued commemorative stamps bearing their portrait and the legend that they were 'assassinated' by the United States. But those close to the case, even a human rights lawyer who detests the death penalty, remain convinced that the quiet couple who beavered away by day in the machine shop were, by night, agents in a far more murky, more lethal world. 'It is a ghastly and shameful episode' said top Yale law professor Alexander Bickel, 'but I believe they were guilty.' Roy Cohn, the prosecutor, says: 'I feel the guilt was proven overwhelmingly and has stood the test of time.'

Only one man's conscience and heart was not touched by the deaths of the Rosenbergs. For Joe the electrician it was just another job, albeit a celebrated one, among the 137 he carried out before he retired from Sing Sing.

Mata Hari

Mata Hari was the most famous of all women spies, using beauty, seduction, and sexuality to squeeze secrets from men who might have withstood any torture, save that inflicted by a lovely woman's charms.

Mata Hari was born in the Dutch town of Leeuwarden on 7 August 1876 as Margaretha Geertruida Zelle. She led an ordinary childhood, was an ordinary student and made the same moans that most teenagers do when they long to do more exciting things. For her that excitement meant moving to a teacher's college near Amsterdam when she was eighteen.

But Margaretha quickly tired of studying and, a year later, married an army officer who took her off to Java. It was here that she first heard the native name 'Mata Hari', – meaning 'eye of the day' – the name under which she would sell military secrets and the name under which she would die.

For the next seven years of her marriage, Margaretha lived the life of an upper-class colonial woman. But she was a woman acutely aware of her own beauty. In Java she started the dalliances which proved to her that her seductive charms could win her anything she wanted. Her husband found out about her affairs but played the part of a cuckolded husband well. He tolerated Margaretha's infidelity for a number of years before taking her back to Holland where they separated and later divorced.

Margaretha found herself with little money in 1902 and so decided to take up the one thing that had been attractive to her as a teenage girl – dancing. She was a very provocative professional and the dancing was strictly for men only. However, Paris was the place to be in cabaret so, in 1905, she moved to the French capital to continue her dancing – and her affairs.

It was there that she adopted the name Mata Hari, that she had first heard used in Java. History is blurred on her days in Paris, but papers released by French authorities last year showed she had many lovers, most of them military officers. Such dalliances were to damn her when the Great War arrived and the world was divided into armed camps. She stayed in Paris for two years after 1914, as the Kaiser's forces were locked in stalemate with the allied armies on a broad front stretching from the channel ports to the frontier of Switzerland.

In 1916 Mata Hari moved back to The Hague, in neutral Holland, – and it was there that she moved into espionage. She fell into the bed of a German diplomat who asked her for details of the French armies in two vital sectors; one was the Somme front where an Anglo–French offensive was expected. The other was at Verdun, which had been heavily fortified and ringed by steel and concrete constructions. The diplomat promised her cash.

The French were later to allege that Mata Hari gleaned the secrets of the French strengths from her lovers in the French Army. What is known is that she was betrayed to the French authorities in 1917 after she had gone to Paris to pass on some intelligence about French battle plans to a Prussian officer. In a war which was bleeding France, she was tried, sentenced to death by a military court and executed on 15 October 1917 by a firing squad.

What were the secrets that she had passed on? Certainly news of Verdun and the Somme offensive could be deemed to be damaging to the war effort of the allied nations. But European capitals were full of agents, and the Somme offensive was certainly no secret to the Germans who knew about it months before it began. Who was it who betrayed Mata Hari?

Since 1917 historians have been puzzled about the whole affair – particularly the French government's refusal to allow public scrutiny of papers sealed in 1917 about Mata Hari. But in 1985 a US journalist, Russell Warren Howe claimed he was shown the secret papers of the spy lady Mata Hari at the Chateau de Vincennes – the very place where she was executed. He claims that the papers show she was not a German agent, but a freelance 'operative' whose sole espionage effort was in Madrid working for the French. Howe says she seduced a German military attaché there and spent three days in bed

Mata Hari in an unusually demure pose.

with him, but the information she got was stale or inaccurate.

Howe claims she did accept money from German intelligence, but all she gave them were easily culled newspaper reports and old gossip. But France in the Great War was rife with anti-foriegn sentiments and had suffered appalling losses which at one time threatened to break the army. Inept generals were to blame, but a scapegoat in the form of a conniving woman seemed a far better bet, argues Howe. At her trial she was charged with peddling secrets which cost the lives of hundreds of thousands of allied servicemen. And the Germans – who believed that Mata Hari had cheated them as a double agent – sent messages in a code which they knew the French had broken implicating her in the espionage charges.

Whichever story is true – that she was a German spy, a French spy or both – Mata Hari broke the ground rules of espionage in that she was indiscreet and naïve enough to think that her bed-hopping would not alert informers. Who actually informed on her is, to this day, still a secret.

Chapter Three

SECRETS OF THE HEART

Love makes men murder, rulers give up their thrones and has made politicans compromise brilliant careers – read on to find out if the lovely Lady Diana Delves Broughton took the secret of her lover's murder to the grave; were President Kennedy and his brother Bobby bedding the greatest sex symbol of the age?; and why was a King's love affair kept from his subjects for so long...?

The Murder In Happy Valley

There was plenty of belt-tightening and digging for victory in wartime Britain as the embattled island braved German bombers and the threat of all-out invasion. In 1940 in particular, the prospects of the tiny British Isles fighting a prolonged war seemed grim indeed. Merchant ships bringing vital supplies into home ports ran a terrifying gauntlet of U-boat wolf packs which daily inflicted greater and greater losses. Everyone from office girls to shopworkers were engaged in war work. There were no luxuries to be had in the shops, nothing to look forward to except a pitifully small meat allowance and dried eggs.

But over 3,000 miles from Britain's shores there was a place where the war was hardly even a distraction; where living was luxurious, riotous, flamboyant, drunken and debauched. In this place the love lives of the inhabitants were matched only by their unquenchable thirsts for fine champagne and rare brandy. In the beautiful countryside of Kenya, one of Imperial Britain's finest colonial possessions, existed a privileged clique of expatriates who turned one of the country's most splendid regions into their own enclave of hedonism. They were the Happy Valley Set and, until murder most foul interrupted their sordid, cocaine-snorting, sex-filled lives, they caroused and partied with a determination probably unmatched since the days of the Romans.

Happy Valley was situated in the White Highlands of Kenya near to the Wanjohi River, not far from the capital of Nairobi. It was splendid country where tobacco and coffee, along with cattle and sheep, were raised by the wealthy colonials who settled there. But Happy Valley seemed destined to attract more than its fair share of scoundrels and rogues than other Empire outposts. The 'Little England', replete with country clubs like the Muthaiga Club, with its well-stocked bars and spacious bedrooms, cultivated a lifestyle among exiled aristocrats which – while pleasurable – was guaranteed one day to end in tragedy. Act One of that tragedy, which unfolded like a Shakespearean love drama, came with the arrival in Happy Valley of Josslyn Hay, the thirty nine-year-old Earl of Erroll and High Constable of Scotland.

Josslyn Hay dedicated his life to philandering with other peoples' wives and had his very own personal motto: 'To Hell with Husbands!' He dressed in

Savile Row-tailored evening suits and smoked cigarettes which bore his personal monogram. As a thoroughly black sheep – expelled from Eton, cited in a British divorce court where the judge called him 'a very bad blackguard' – Kenya offered this accomplished womanizer and seducer rich pickings. It was also, cynics suspected, a 'cushy' spot for the recently enlisted Hay who landed the post of Military Secretary there – well away from the bombs and deprivations of the home front. Kenya was the focal point for mustering British forces planning the assault on Italian-occupied Ethiopia. Apart from memo writing and answering to higher command, there was little for Josslyn Hay to do except womanize – the thing that he was most expert at.

Hay would probably have sat out the war and died comfortably many years later with a gin in his hand and a woman at his side if a certain Diana Delves Broughton, the beautiful bride of Sir Henry Delves Broughton, had not entered the Happy Valley enclave. Diana, twenty six, arrived with Sir Henry – known as Jock to his friends – in November 1940. Formerly Diana Caldwell, she had married a man thirty years her senior after meeting him at a race meeting in England. He was newly divorced and they married at the end of October and were in Kenya within a week. Sir Henry had opted for life in the colony for several reasons, but mostly because he was struggling financially and planned a last-ditch venture raising cattle there. Everyone who knew him was aware that horse racing was the greatest love of his life – and he embraced it with a passion that cost him untold thousands. He still had money, but not enough to live as wildly as he once had. His savings, though, would guarantee a gracious life in Kenya.

The marriage with Diana was a strange one from the outset. Diana was both beautiful and young and Jock was old – and ageing fast. He knew that for him the marriage was a bond of companionship more than anything else. Those who knew him said they sensed a certain fatalism about him, that it was as if he knew he could not hold on to his ravishing young wife for long. But not even he thought that their marriage would flounder literally within weeks of stepping into the African sunshine.

On 30 November 1940, the sparkling eyes of Diana met those of Josslyn Hay across the bar of the Muthaiga Club – and she fell in love instantly. She had already heard of Josslyn Hay's reputation as a seducer; as a man who derived as much pleasure from seeing the cuckolded husbands squirm as he did from making love to their wives. None the less, there was a genuine sexual chemistry between the two. Josslyn Hay calmly walked over to her and, she was later to recall, spoke these first words to her: 'Well, who's going to tell Jock, you or I?'

Hay, who had been married twice before – his first marriage ending in divorce, his second wife dying from drinking and drugs – courted Diana

The Earl of Erroll and Lady Diana Delves Broughton.

shamelessly in front of the exiled aristocrats. They flaunted their affection at tea dances, dinners, cocktail parties and club banquets. If they tried to keep it from the one person who could claim a right to know – Jock – they didn't make a very good job of it. He knew he was being made a fool of by a younger man, but did little to change the situation. It was even brought to his attention by anonymous letters left in his pigeon hole at the Muthaiga Club. Two months after the affair had begun, on 6 January 1941, an unsigned note left for him read: 'You seemed like a cat on hot bricks last night. What about the eternal triangle? What are you going to do about it?' Some days later a friend who sat next to the elderly Jock as he sipped gin slings at the Muthaiga, watching his wife and Hay dance, whispered to him: 'Do you know that Joss is madly in love with Diana?' It is inconceivable that Jock could not help but know, especially as just twelve days later another anonymous note in his pigeon hole informed him that Diana had spent a weekend with Joss at a friend's home in Nyeri; expeditions which Diana had told Jock were 'girls only' outings to swim and watch big game.

There are conflicting reports about what kind of man Sir Henry Delves

Broughton was. Some say he was an outlandish snob with a contempt of anyone born out of his social sphere; others that he was a kindly old gent who asked for little more than some ready cash to spend on his beloved horses and a wife to give him a little companionship in his old age. An old Etonian – like his rival in love (only he wasn't expelled) – Jock exemplified the stiff-upper-lip attitude of the British everywhere when confronted with an unpleasant situation. He said nothing, perhaps in the misguided notion that his wife's fling with Joss Hay was no more than girlish affection. But on 18 January, the same day as Jock received the second note, Diana went to him and told him she was leaving him for Hay.

In a pathetic attempt to win his wife back he asked her to accompany him on a three month cruise to Ceylon so she could reconsider her decision. Then in a move which showed his utter grasp of unreality about the whole affair, he said she could take Joss with them if it pleased her! Diana had no intention of changing her mind or going on the cruise; she used the pretext that Joss was too busily engaged in war work to go off around the world, and she was certainly going nowhere without her lover. The following day Hay presented Diana with a string of pearls and on 20 January Diana walked out on Jock.

Sombre Jock watched his wife drive out of the estate gates for the last time. If he was upset, he did not show it to the staff, but rather set to work in a bid to erase the pain he must have been feeling.

The following day, 21 January, he telephoned the police to say that burglars had entered the house at night and had stolen two revolvers – both in his possession since his First World War service – some cash and a cigarette case. After completing formalities with police officers, he went to see a lawyer about getting a divorce. Then he penned a letter to a friend in England: 'They say they are in love with each other and mean to get married. It is a hopeless position and I am going to cut my losses. I think I'll go to Ceylon. There's nothing for me in Kenya any longer.'

Two days after that, the few British people of the Happy Valley set who did not indulge in the sordid revels beloved by the majority of the region rallied round 'poor old Jock'. He was invited to tea by a close friend, Mrs Carberry. Unfortunately, Diana and Hay were there too, invited by a third party. But there were no challenges to a duel. Sir Henry Delves Broughton behaved impeccably towards them both. In fact he was such a model of civility and charm that Hay later remarked to a friend: 'Jock could not have been nicer. He has agreed to go away. As a matter of fact he has been so nice it smells bad.'

That evening there was more generosity of spirit from Jock. At a club party where the affair had ceased to be a secret months ago, Jock raised his champagne glass and said: 'I wish them every happiness. May their union be blessed with an heir. To Diana and Joss.' The glasses were clinked and the Happy Valley hedonists echoed the words of Jock as they toasted the lovers.

Three hours later Lord Erroll, philanderer, scoundrel, wife-stealer, was dead – his brains blown out by point-blank pistol shots to the head.

Sir Henry Delves Broughton had staggered to his bed, much the worse for drink, at 2.00 a.m. the morning after the party. Lord Errol had promised that he would bring Diana home to spend one more night under Jock's roof – Jock's last request before Diana walked out of his life forever. He arrived at the mansion in his Buick and delivered Diana safely at 2.15 a.m. At 3.00 a.m. Lord Erroll was found dead, slumped beneath the dashboard of the car which had left the road four kilometres from Delves Broughton's home and had plunged into a pit. He was discovered by two labourers walking along the Nairobi-Ngong road and had been shot at point blank range with a .32 revolver. Two hours later the news was broken to Jock and Diana. The former took it with a look of stunned disbelief – Diana was so distraught she had to be sedated.

But what the police failed to tell them was how Hay died. They let Jock and Diana think that they believed that Hay met his end in a straightforward road accident. The police had already pinpointed Jock as their chief suspect – he had motive, means and willpower to commit murder – and wanted twenty four hours to gather evidence before bringing charges.

The following day Diana, still hazy from the sedatives which had been pumped into her to calm her down, gave a scented handkerchief to Jock and told him to drive to the morgue in Nairobi and place it on Hay's body. Bemused, he did so, handing it to a guard, saying: 'Please place this on his body would you? My wife was very much in love with Lord Erroll.'

In the afternoon there was a bonfire in Jock's garden – numerous articles were consigned to the flames after being doused with petrol. Only one charred artefact survived – a bloodstained Argyll sock. On 25 January, just as Lord Erroll's coffin was being lowered into the ground, the police announced publicly in Kenya that he had not been the unfortunate victim of a road crash, but of a cold-blooded killer. They revealed what they believed was the scenario; that a man had either flagged the car down, or had been sitting next to Hay, when he forced the car to slow down and fired the fatal shots. The car was then pushed off the road with the dying Earl pushed under the dashboard. The implication for Diana was inescapable – her cuckolded husband had killed her lover. The champagne toast and the wishes of good luck were all a cruel trick. Jock had committed murder.

It was the same conclusion drawn by the police, although Jock was not formally charged with the murder until 10 March. For the most part, there was great sympathy for the aristocratic old gentleman – but also a great deal of surprise, not to say astonishment, when Diana suddenly flew to Johannesburg to hire the best criminal lawyer in Africa to defend him! Jock came to trial in June and it was a sensation for the newspapers. Weary of reporting depressing news about the bombing, blackout and rationing, the steamy scandal was played out in the full glare of publicity for a public hungry for such intriguing revelations.

The case against Jock was this; that he had the motive to kill Hay, that bullets found near his home at a practice shooting range matched those found at the murder scene and that the bonfire, which failed to consume the bloodstained sock, was set to burn clothes which he mistakenly splashed with blood during the killing. The prosecution alleged that the toast to the good health of Hay and Diana was a sham, perpetrated only to hide Jock's real intent – murder. It was alleged that far from being drunk on champagne, Jock had merely feigned his boozy state, slipping out later to intercept the car – knowing that Hay would stop – and then killing him.

Harry Morris, the brilliant South African lawyer hired to represent Jock by his wife, destroyed the most vital piece of police evidence – the gun theory – by bringing in an expert who testified that there was no way the bullets which killed Hay could have been fired from Jock's gun. Moreover, the murder weapon had not been found. As for the bonfire – what was the significance of one blood-stained sock, so badly charred that the blood was unuseable for forensic examination?

For his part, Sir Henry performed magnificently in the witness box. He already had that most valuable ally – public opinion – on his side, and with his gracious manner and stern denial of foul play, won the jury's heart.

On 1 July 1941 Jock emerged into Nairobi's bright sunshine a free man after the jury unanimously found him not guilty.

Whodunnit? Through the years the Happy Valley murder has remained an enigma that could, possibly, have been answered by only one person – Diana herself. But she died in 1987, rich, extravagant and secretive to the last. Did she know who pulled the trigger? Certainly, she patched up, to an extent, her relationship with Jock after the trial. They did take the cruise to Ceylon after all, although halfway through he fell hard on the deck, badly injuring his back. The injury left him with partial paralysis and he returned to England while Diana eventually made her way back to Kenya. Sir Henry commited suicide, in 1942 in Liverpool, leaving notes in which he said the strain of the trial, and ensuing publicity, was too much to bear.

June Carberry, who invited Jock to the tea at her place only to find Hay and Diana showing up too, testified at his trial that she had stayed in his home the night the murder was commited, and believed he could not have done it because he was so drunk. But now, at sixty three, her daughter Juanita has come forward with a claim that Jock confessed all to her when she was a fifteen year old schoolgirl. She said she caught him burning the bloodstained clothing and he told her: 'I hate Happy Valley and its people.' She added: 'I felt a great loyalty to him and I didn't think he was criminal or wicked. I thought he was a lonely distraught man who needed a friend. And I felt very grown up that he trusted me. He killed him.'

But another theory is that one of Hay's ex-mistresses – who killed one of her lovers in Paris five years previously – may have made the journey to Africa to settle an old score. Alice de Janze was known to be consumed by fiery jealousies that could have made such a scheme possible. On the other hand, perhaps the killer was Diana – sensing perhaps that she too could have been ditched by the fanatically unfaithful Earl like others before her.

Whatever she knew, it was a secret that she would take to the grave.

The King and Mrs Simpson

Edward, Prince of Wales, nurtured the secret close to his heart for months. He had fallen for a woman that his position as monarch would never allow him to marry. And yet, hopelessly and obsessively, he could not end the affair – preferring instead to abandon his throne in order to keep the affections of Wallis Simpson. But for the British people, the Prince's love affair was kept secret. While abroad people snickered over the weak Edward's little-boy-lost love for the divorced Simpson, censors and the British establishment combined to keep the very people he reigned over in the dark about their King's lover. It was a calculated move designed to keep an entire nation cut off from reality. It was hardly surprising, therefore, that once the secret was out, it engulfed Edward, Wallis, the establishment and the monarchy like a tidal wave.

Edward VIII was King of Great Britain for 326 days before he abdicated for the woman he loved. But he had been blindly in love for nearly three years with Wallis Simpson. The object of His Majesty's desire in 1936 was the lady who he had met in 1931, a witty but rather plain thirty four year-old American, who had had a childhood and upbringing just about as far as one could get from the House of Windsor. Her father, a businessman from Maryland, had died when she was just five months old and she had been raised in Baltimore by her mother. She married a Navy pilot in 1916, confessing that she found the combination of uniform and derring-do a thrilling combination. But the union with Earl Winfield Spencer was short lived and they were separated in 1922. Her second marriage came in 1928 to Ernest Simpson, a respectable businessman, half British, half American, who headed the London Office of his family's shipping company. It was his arrival in Britain in 1929 that thrust Wallis Simpson on to the London social scene. It had always been an ambition of her mother's that Wallis should elevate herself within society, leaving behind the low social order and poverty of her upbringing. With marriage to Ernest she seemed to have accomplished her goal and established a reputation among the rich and privileged set of the time as something of an amusing and competent hostess. She moved among diplomats, lords and ladies – and loved it. However as Wallis began to enjoy the London social whirl more and more, she began to find her husband staid, dull and uninteresting.

It was in December 1930 that the new first secretary at the American Embassy, Benjamin Thaw, was invited to dinner at the Simpsons'. He came with his wife Consuelo, and her sister Thelma, Viscountess Furness. Lady Furness, a vampish beauty with affected Hollywood starlet looks and manners, had her own secret; she was mistress to the Prince of Wales. A friendship burgeoned between the three women, with Thelma confiding to Wallis about her secret love. Eventually, the Simpsons dined with the Prince and were soon regular visitors to his country retreat. He too dined at the Simpsons' flat off Oxford Street. In January 1934 the Viscountess, at a dinner party, discreetly said to Wallis Simpson: 'I am making a trip to the United States. Please would you look after the Prince to make sure he isn't lonely?' Wallis looked after him all right, rather a little too well for Thelma's liking. By the time she returned in the spring, Wallis and the Prince were lovers.

The secret of the relationship was shared by a small elite group. In the 1930s the Press was far more conservative and did not employ the kind of professional 'royal watchers' of today whose sole tasks are reporting trivia and intimate details of the House of Windsor. Conversely, Edward was being sucked into an emotional vortex which would run directly contrary to his responsibilities as the future King of Great Britain. The secret love letters, which were released after Wallis Simpson's death at the age of eighty nine in 1986, showed the bizarre mother-son relationship which the couple shared – even though Wallis was in fact two years younger than the Prince. His letters are full of infantile pleading, a need to be re-assured, cosseted, adoring in his affections for her. Hers are admonishing, stern, sensible, possessive.

The privileged group of friends who in the early days witnessed them together say that he was completely captivated by her. She, slender, sophisticated, poised, elegant and witty, was the exact opposite of the rather boyish would-be King of Great Britain.

It is not known at which exact date the Prince told the royal family of his love for Wallis Simpson – but they could well have learned from the Prince's indiscreet flaunting of his new mistress on trips to Paris, the French Riviera, Budapest, Berlin and Italy. The foreign press had a field day. Detailed accounts of their trysts in romantic hotels were published in every language from French to Finnish and even the United States press came in on the act – calling Wallis, 'Queen Wally'! Amazingly, Fleet Street printed not a word. The newspapers then were owned by the powerful press barons, men like Rothermere and Beaverbrook, who saw it as their duty to preserve the façade of the British Monarchy – even if their future king were behaving like a playboy. Newspapers coming into the country from overseas had references to the liaison removed and the British public remained ignorant of Edward's behaviour with a twice-divorced woman. The US press in particular went to town with photographs and a story about the couple's visits to Yugoslavia, Greece and Turkey.

Edward became King Edward VIII in December 1935. The affair was at its height and the love letters from Edward to Wallis became ever more sloppy and infantile. But Edward still had the British establishment on his side – that curious creature which is capable of so much indiscretion as long as it is discreet. For Edward and Wallis that turning point was reached when the secret was out on 3 December 1936. Some weeks before then Wallis had finally received a divorce from her husband. Prime Minister Stanley Baldwin, who knew then of the entanglement that Edward had with Wallis, asked the king to persuade Wallis not to go through with the divorce. But Edward told him: 'I have no right to interfere with the affairs of an individual. It would be wrong were I to attempt to influence Mrs Simpson just because she happens to be a friend of the king.' Secretly, it was what he wished and conspired for – knowing that in six months time, before his coronation, he would be free to wed her.

The conspiracy of silence ended when the Bishop of Bradford, Dr Blunt, publicly chastised Edward for his carefree lifestyle which he said was incongruous with a man who was the head of the British Empire. The newspapers construed that the Bishop's outburst was aimed directly at the relationship between the king and Wallis Simpson. The secret was out. Edward was swamped by the public reaction to his affair and naïvely believed that the establishment and the people would understand his affair of the heart. But there would be no sympathetic tears shed for his blighted love. Queen Mary, his mother, was outraged and sent for Baldwin to attend Buckingham Palace. Edward had hoped to move Baldwin into accepting Wallis as his bride and, therefore, as the future Queen. Edward had not yet had his coronation and he believed his popularity with the British people would win through and he would be allowed to marry Wallis. Baldwin told him: 'We will not have it sir. People are talking about you and this American woman. I have had so many nasty letters from people who respected your father and who do not appreciate the way you are going on.'

In the eight days between revelation and abdication, Wallis was subjected to a fearful hate campaign. Stones were hurled through the window of her London home and she received hurtful letters. The children were later to sing in the streets: 'Hark the Herald Angels Sing, Mrs Simpson's pinched our King.' Wallis fled to the South of France while Edward battled against the established order and his own feelings. He was told to ditch Wallis and to assume the responsibilities to which his whole life had been leading, like a man. He tried to sway various influential politicians and press barons, but without much success. One in whom he found an ally was Winston Churchill who, at a lunch with playwright Noel Coward remarked: 'Why shouldn't the king marry his cutie?' 'Because', remarked Coward, 'England does not want a Queen Cutie.' Finally Edward approached the publisher of the *Daily Mail*, Esmond Harmsworth, who suggested the idea of a morganatic marriage – once popular in German royal states – whereby Wallis could become his bride, but would not assume the title of Queen. Her children similarly would have no rights to the throne of Great Britain. Wallis begrudgingly accepted the idea, but it was to no avail; the cabinet would not entertain the idea. If Edward were to remain as king, it would be without Wallis Simpson at his side.

The king, hopelessly, blindly in love with Wallis, decided to abdicate and resolve the constitutional crisis looming over Britain. When Wallis heard that he had stepped down from the throne on 11 December, and broadcast his message to the British people the following night, she wept. Later in her memoirs she wrote: 'I was lying on the sofa with my hands over my eyes, trying to hide my tears.' The King had told the nation that he could not rule without the woman he loved by his side. Edward then left for France, never again to set foot on the shores of his beloved Great Britain.

The couple lived in a splendid white château on the outskirts of Paris for which they paid a peppercorn rent. They married in the Loire Valley and remained as distant outcasts from the Royal family until their deaths – he in May 1972 aged seventy seven, she fourteen years later.

Only at Edward's funeral at St George's Chapel, Windsor, did Wallis come to see the members of the royal family that she so wished to join. She spent one night in Buckingham Palace before returning to her exile in Paris. She ended her days lonely, bedridden, a sad figure whose secret affaire burgeoned into one of the classic romantic tragedies of the century. On her dressing room table she kept a framed message penned by Edward, who assumed the title of Duke of Windsor after his abdication. The touching lines read: 'My friend, with thee to live alone, methinks were better than to own, a crown, a sceptre and a throne.'

Baby Love

In 1986 scandal split the Anglican Church in the United States. It was in the shape of a little bundle of joy named Evan. Evan is now a healthy little girl who plays happily in the garden of her home without a care in the world – and she certainly has no inkling that her birth took place in a storm of publicity. For Evan was born to an unmarried woman priest – a priest, moreover, who conceived her baby not just out of wedlock – but from artificial insemination, from not one but three donors! Now the church hierarchy is threatening that it the mother does not reveal the father's identity she will face excommunication.

The Reverend Lesley Northup was brought up in a religious family in Washington. From her earliest days she attended Sunday school and was fascinated both by the ritual of the Church and the values which its message of love and compassion instilled in her. Lesley Northup's mind was firmly made up; she was going to spread the word of the Lord when she grew up. In 1981 she was ordained by the Bishop of New York, the Right Reverend Paul

Moore. He announced to the assembled congregation that Lesley Northup had the 'qualities and dignity' of a woman well suited to the calling of Christ.

But Reverend Northup had another, equally strong calling – to become a mother. She said: 'I knew that my life was devoted to God and I didn't want a husband because I was so devoted to the Church. But there were feelings within me that I would like to be a mother. To give life, to nurture it and watch it grow. That seemed important to me and did not veer from the teachings of the Bible. I know that the pathway I was considering was not a very romantic one, but it was morally correct. I have no regrets.'

What Lesley did was to enlist the help of two fellow sympathetic male priests and another church worker. They each agreed to provide sperm for artifical insemination. 'I chose them because they were healthy and relatively stable,' said Lesley. 'Good looks didn't count and there was no adultery because they were all single. I was determined that no one, including myself, should know the identity of the father. So on three consecutive nights at my home I artifically inseminated myself. The results are to be found in the beautiful form of my baby daughter.'

Lesley did not foresee the strength of protest and indignation that rose up to meet her when Evan was born. Aside from Church outrage, she was the target of a vicious and prolonged campaign of abuse from the public. Her home was the target of vandals and one letter to her read: 'You have sinned against the Lord. You are an abomination to the church you claim to represent, whore! You will fry in hell.'

Lesley was stunned by the public reaction. She said: 'I did nothing wrong and yet this was happening to me. I didn't want a baby to be the result of a promiscuous act and I didn't want anyone to think that. People said to me: "If you want a baby so badly why don't you just get married?" But you don't just wake up one day and say: "I'll go to the supermarket today and get a husband." And you don't get married just to have a baby. When I got pregnant I didn't want any of the donors to feel responsible individually, but when Evan was born I received christening gifts from all of them. Judging by her looks I have no idea who her father is. She had the bad taste – but the good sense – to resemble a small clone of her mother, so both the donor anonymity and my exclusive parental rights have been protected.'

'Now if I happen to meet one of them, they ask me how she is, but that is all. I couldn't have done this without men but I would point out that I am not a radical feminist. I have gone out with men, I have had relationships with men. I have no anti-male bias whatsoever. I have a quiet, middle-class life and I really am rather conservative in my politics. I chose artifical insemination because it would have been dishonest to get married just to have a baby – plus I devote too much time to God.'

73

The Reverend Lesley Northup with baby Evan.

Lesley admits that finding the men for the undertaking was a tricky business – especially as she stipulated that they were not to have any involvement with the child's upbringing. But the greatest problems facing her stem from the Church establishment in the United States. She has been the subject of countless debates and the latest dictate from her bishops demand that she reveal the father before they move on to decide what is to become of her. But Lesley is adamant – the secret of the donors will stay just that. Eve the local Bishop who ordained her, has gone against church thinking to declare his support for her. He said: 'There was no adultery and there were no grounds to depose her. So I came out and said: "OK, I am right behind you." I have no intention of criticizing her or condemning her. I couldn't tell her not to have the baby. When you get down to it, she wanted to bring up her own child and I felt she could do a great job. I looked over the Ten Commandments and I didn't see that she had broken any of them."

But his view is not shared by many more othodox, right-wing clerics in the church hierarchy. One of her most outspoken critics, the Reverend John Yates of Vermont, said: 'Her decision to produce a child through artificial insemination is another indicator of the discouraging, dehumanizing drift in our society's perceptions of parenthood and family life. Many in the church do not think she belongs in the cloth and I would support that view.'

Lesley continues to show that she is a force to be reckoned with, declaring: 'I am so proud of what I have done I won't even keep the truth from Evan. How it's phrased will depend on when she asks, but certainly she'll get the whole truth. And she may have a brother or sister to ask as well – because I would certainly have no qualms about doing it again.'

The President and Marilyn Monroe

For almost fifty years the United State's domestic crime agency the FBI was ruled with an iron fist by J. Edgar Hoover, a man possessed by huge prejudice, intense paranoia and an obsession with other people's sex lives. Widely rumoured to be a homosexual himself, Hoover took on a crusading zeal whenever he found what he considered immoral or indecent behaviour in others. Hoover always looked for weaknesses in his real or imagined enemies and built up files which gave him immense potential power over them. For years his twisted brain consumed and collated information ready to be put to use – and no public figure had a bigger personal file within Hoover's office than the President of the United States of America himself – the charismatic John F. Kennedy.

Charismatic Kennedy was anathema to the things which reactionary Hoover believed in. Always hunting communists and liberals, Hoover despised the Kennedy reforms of the racist school system in the southern states and his links with black leader Martin Luther King. Consequently Hoover set out to discover the weaknesses of John F. Kennedy. He found them not in booze, or pornography, bribery, civic corruption or money. Kennedy's weakness was sex.

He had many illicit affairs during his marriage to his wife Jacqueline, both before he stepped into the White House and after. However, unknown to Kennedy at the start of his tenure of office, Hoover had placed many key White House personnel on the FBI payroll as his personal stooges within the President's official residence. Kennedy's telephone conversations were taped, the meetings he had with women secretly watched with times, dates and places being meticulously recorded. Kennedy's attraction to and for other women was something that revolted Hoover. But something that has remained a mystery to this day is whether Kennedy had an affair with the most sexual woman of the age – Marilyn Monroe. And not only him, but his brother Robert Kennedy, was also widely rumoured to have shared the bed of the sex symbol who seemingly killed herself with barbiturates in August 1962 at the age of thirty six. Since her death over a quarter of a century ago, the ghost of Marilyn Monroe has never been laid to rest. Many theories have

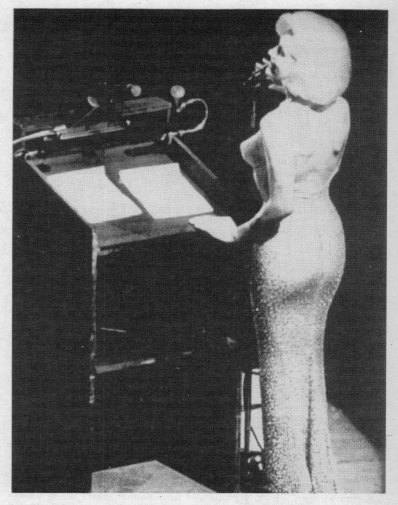

Marilyn singing at President Kennedy's birthday party.

surfaced – ugly stories that the death has not a suicide after all.

Marilyn's affair with President Kennedy was said to have been known by all, but discussed by none. And her death, some allege, was brought about because she intended to publicly expose her affair with the president. There have been other bizarre theories: Did mobsters bug the star's bedroom in a bid to blackmail the Kennedys who were cracking down hard on organized crime? Did Robert Kennedy, then Attorney General in the US, break off his relationship with Marilyn on the very day she died? Did the Kennedys' brother-in-law, the actor Peter Lawford, destroy a suicide note from Marilyn that may have leaked the sensational news that she bedded the two most powerful men in the United States? Was she murdered in a move guaranteed to keep her silent? No serious investiagation has ever placed such a crime at the doorstep of the Kennedys – but several noted journalists who have probed the suicide story believe that mafia bosses – sick of the war waged on them by the Kennedys – may have decided to fake Marilyn's suicide in order to lure Robert Kennedy into a trap.

If the stories are true that both Kennedy brothers indulged in affairs with Marilyn Monroe, the suspicions over her death will continue to linger for many years to come.

Jeanne Martin, ex-wife of singer Dean Martin, is one who claims that Lawford, who was married to Kennedy sister Patricia, played 'pimp' for the Kennedy brothers in fixing up dates with Marilyn. She says: 'I saw Peter in the role of pimp for Jack Kennedy. It was a nasty business.' Jeanne, who does admit never to have actually seen Jack or Bobby Kennedy in bed with Marilyn, added that she does feel 'quite sure' that both men were sleeping with the star.

Other sources say that John Kennedy frequently had rendezvous with Marilyn in a plush New York Hotel. Jane Shalam, the daughter of an influential political family in the city, said she frequently saw Marilyn leaving and entering the hotel by the rear entrance at a time she knew Kennedy was staying inside. Singer Phyllis McGuire, of the McGuire Sisters, says: 'The initial relationship was with John. And there definitely was a relationship afterwards with Bobby. They were seen together at their little hideaways. And, you know, that's very like the Kennedys, to pass it down from one to the other.' Another source claims that President Kennedy 'passed her on' when he grew fearful of Hoover's investigations into his private life – and made sure that Robert always used a false name when speaking with Marilyn on a telephone which was equipped with a special scrambler to prevent wiretapping by Hoover's agents.

Actress Jeanne Carmen, a friend and neighbour of Marilyn's in Hollywood, claims she was witness to an astonishing episode at Marilyn's Los

Angeles apartment in the autumn of 1961. She said: 'I was at Marilyn's place once evening when the doorbell rang. She was in the tub and she called me to get it. I opened the door and there was Bobby. He had that expression when he saw me of not knowing whether to run, walk or stay. I was stunned and kept saying, "come in, come in". Finally I got out of his way and Marilyn came flying out of the bathroom, and jumped into his arms. She kissed him openly, which was out of character for her.' Carmen also says that Bobby Kennedy and the movie queen enjoyed a naked romp on a nudist beach near Malibu – Marilyn dressed up in a wig and he wearing a fake beard.

One of Lawford's ex-wives, Deborah Gould, said the affair with Jack Kennedy began before he took office in 1961. He broke it off, allegedly because he found Marilyn 'dangerously talkative'. Initially Bobby was just used as the messenger boy, says Gould, but then he found himself spellbound by her beauty and sexuality. But Lawford, who died in 1984, repeatedly and vehemently denied that the affairs had ever taken place. His denial of the secret trysts is not believed by investigative journalist Anthony Summers who, in his book about Marilyn called *Goddess*, speculates: 'It seems that for many months she engaged in intermittent sexual encounters with both the President and Robert Kennedy. For both the brothers and for Marilyn, there had been an initial attraction between stars, each glittering prizes in the interlocking galaxies of politics and show business. The Kennedy brothers, bred to the knowledge that they could have any woman they desired, at first failed to perceive that in Marilyn Monroe they were dealing with a woman who was doubly dangerous.'

Summers says that the nature of the 'danger' lay in the fact that she represented a threat to both of their political lives. She was despondent over frequent miscarriages and abortions – the result of a string of failed love affairs – and her fading movie career. Her grip on reality was ebbing away too.

On the night she died, Summers speculates that Peter Lawford, who was the last person to speak to her on the telephone, came to Marilyn's house before she was dead and, possibly with Robert Kennedy there, took the dying actress to a hospital in Santa Monica. However, when Monroe died, the corpse was rushed back to her home and the death scene was staged before the police were called. His book makes no firm charge, but leaves open the possibility that 'someone else administered the fatal overdose'.

Milo Speriglio, head of a private detective agency in Los Angeles, has been fascinated with Marilyn Monroe, her apparent liaison with the Kennedys and her untimely death ever since she was found in the cold light of day on 5 August all those years ago. He is convinced she was murdered.

Speriglio says he began with a re-investigation of the inquest and police reports. The coroner ruled suicide after hearing that she had swallowed forty-seven capsules of barbiturates. But the autopsy stated that the stomach was almost completely empty except for a small residue of brownish liquid. Also no water was found in her stomach. Did she take forty-seven pills without any water? Sergeant Jack Clemmons, the police officer first at the scene in her home in the LA suburb of Brentwood, noticed that there was no vomit around – usually the first sign that someone has tried suicide with pills – no glass, no water. Jack Clemmons has now left the force and told Speriglio he had recommended an investigation to his superiors. He was told to totally forget about the idea.

Speriglio claims that a friend of Monroe's, Robert Slatzer, first alerted him to the murder theory. Slatzer had known Marilyn for sixteen years and claimed she had told him about her affairs with the Kennedy brothers. Slatzer claimed she showed him a red diary containing the red-hot accounts of her lovemaking liaisons with the brothers and other significant people. He believed that the diary was a reason for her murder. Speriglio says that Monroe actually believed that Bobby Kennedy was going to leave his wife and his large family for her. 'When Robert tried to dump her too like his brother had done, she behaved like a scorned woman,' said Speriglio. 'He had broken up with her in a ruthless way, by having the private phone line on which she called him disconnected.'

Speriglio tried to get copies of Marilyn's phone bills – numbers dialled which would have been listed on the bill – but he found they had apparently gone 'missing'. He tried to find the diary which had been passed into the custody of deputy coroner's aide Lionel Grandison who signed Marilyn's death certificate. Speriglio claimed Grandison told him he had looked through the book and seen references to the Kennedys and some mafia figures in San Diego. But when Speriglio returned the next day with a request to see the diary, the book had not only gone – but had also been struck from the inventory of personal effects turned over to the state.

The private eye also says he had evidence that the Monroe home was bugged – one of his sources was Bernard Spindel, an expert wiretapper who was arrested by the FBI in 1966 and who died in prison before Speriglio could get his hands on the tapes he possessed. But before he died he filed a petition to the Supreme Court citing return of 'a confidential file containing tapes and evidence concerning circumstances surrounding the death of Marilyn Monroe which strongly suggests the official reported circumstances of her demise are erroneous.' Speriglio believed from talking to other informants in the Senate that Marilyn was preparing a news conference to get her own back on the Kennedys – spilling the beans not only on their love affairs but the death plots which, Speriglio claims, Kennedy told her about and which were aimed at Cuban dictator Fidel Castro.

Speriglio charges that the CIA – the sometimes unorthodox intelligence agency of the United States – was involved in Marilyn's death, plotters in the bizarre power-play who may have administered a lethal injection of barbiturates to prevent a scandal from engulfing the White House. Speriglio said: 'In 1980 under the Freedom of Information Act, I petitioned the FBI for Marilyn Monroe's file. Most of the material was blanked out and, under orders of FBI director William Webster, eighteen of the forty-three pages were completely witheld. The reason given for the exempted eighteen pages was national defence and foreign policy. The remaining material was useless.

'But I'd like to know just what in the files of a two-decades-dead movie star still threatens national security!'

Eric Clapton and the Chamber Maid

For months the gossip columns had been filled with the news that buzzed across the Atlantic. Eric Clapton, legendary guitarist, musician extraordinaire, a man who beat heroin and booze addictions to produce some of the best rock music ever, was to be a father again. That fact alone wasn't so startling – it was *who* was going to be the mother. Clapton had already raised more than a few music-world eyebrows when his beautiful Italian mistress Lory Del Santo gave birth at the age of twenty six to the singer's son Conor in August 1986. Patti Boyd, thirty eight, who left ex-Beatle George Harrison for Clapton in 1974, and who married him in 1979, named Lory in her divorce petition. When the rumours started buzzing towards the end of the summer of 1987 that Clapton was going to be a father again, the thoughts were not of *when* but of *who* was carrying his child.

As it turned out, neither Lory or Patty were pregnant by Clapton. But out of the shadows of New York's clubland came a part-time singer, part-time chambermaid with a definite bulge under her dress. Alina Moreni, twenty seven, was carrying Eric Clapton's love child – or so she said.

Fleet Street went mad for her story. The bouncy beauty had an amazing yarn to tell of her secret affair. In both British and American newspapers she boasted how fairytale love had blossomed when she met Clapton at a club in Manhattan one night. She said that she lived in one of New York's smartest streets, Park Avenue, with her wealthy mother, and was an Italian Baroness in a self-imposed exile of luxury in the most exciting city she knew. Her life, she sighed, was a tidal wave of champagne and roses, played out against the backdrop of exciting New York. Her story was the stuff of romantic novels. In one interview she said: 'I knew when I fell in love with Eric Clapton that it was never going to be easy. He has a beautiful heart, but not much brains. He thinks with the most intimate part of his body. But underneath all that he's just a playful, insecure child. That's why I have always liked him – and that's one of the things he always liked about me: my honesty.'

Alina's honesty in her interviews was quite breathtaking. She revealed how she and Clapton had a mad passionate fling which resulted in her pregnancy. She said it was a matter of time before Eric made a statement about their love, and also about the matter of paying maintenance for the child which was due to be born in April 1988.

The publicity was certainly paying off for Alina. She was booked to sing in some of the better-known New York nightclubs and boasted proudly of a hurried love-call to Eric every time she was off stage. 'He makes my heart beat with desire', she gushed in a New York newspaper. 'He is just waiting for the day we can be together forever. He, me and our baby. It will be perfect.' Even though she was heavily pregnant, Alina managed to draw the kind of publicity usually reserved for more shapely aspiring crooners. She was snapped by the paparazzi as she left clubs, snapped as she went in, and droned on about the 'special magic' she shared with Eric. 'I am only revealing the secret of our love because he is soon to break the news to Lory,' said Alina. But the real secret was something quite different indeed . . .

Day by day Alina was getting bigger until she resembled a matronly Italian housewife, clasping her hands in front of her to help hold the burden she was carrying. And then one day her manager, Lynne Robinson, who was helping to promote her singing career noticed that the 'pregnancy lump' seemed to move! 'I have seen pregnant women before,' said Lynne, 'and this seemed most odd. The lump definitely shifted – and when I saw her again it seemed to have moved once again.' There was no comment from the Clapton camp about the singer's entangled love life. His management refused to be drawn into the star's personal life.

Then in May, when Alina looked fit to burst, she 'went into hospital to give birth to our darling child'. But while she was away, newspaper men from both sides of the Atlantic began sniffing around what looked like being a very fishy tale indeed. It turned out that Alina was no Italian Baroness. She was a full-time, hard-up maid who last year cleaned the apartment of Eric Clapton. There was no crime in rich and poor getting together in a union of passion, however. Friends rushed to her side to say that the Italian Baroness story was concocted merely to give Eric's friends in the pop world a more favourable impression of his latest love.

But then other cracks began appearing in the saga; Robinson told how she tried to reach out to touch pregnant Alina's stomach, and 'she winced away as if in pain.' She added: 'She wouldn't let me near her. That was when I was convinced that she was a faker and that the whole thing was some kind of calculated sting against Clapton. I said to her: "You are a very, very sick girl and need help." I am a mother of three children and I know how people behave when they are pregnant. There was no way that this woman was carrying anything other than a pillow up her dress.'

Alina's other close friend Rose Genero, who had known her for six years, said Alina telephoned her from a New York hospital on 8 May to say she had given birth to a bouncing baby girl, and that she was going to call her Rosa Lina Clapton. Eric had been on the telephone from London, she told Rose, and everything was fine. 'But I checked back with the hospital and there was no record of her being there or indeed of a baby girl being born that night,' said Rose. 'I think I knew then that the real secret was not her fling with a pop star, but the fact that she had embarked on a Walter Mitty exercise that had only one ending. She was bound to be found out sooner or later. Maybe she did have a fling with Clapton but she sure as hell wasn't carrying his baby.

With pressure from the media building up, Alina went into hiding with her 'baby' – she still insisted that she had given birth and that Eric was on his way to see her. But then two days later she confessed sobbing to Fleet Street reporters: 'I did not have his baby. I had an abortion because I saw the way he was treating me. When I saw his attitude towards me I knew that he had changed. But I am a woman and I am proud. That is why I pretended for so long that I was carrying his child. It was a very upsetting time all round and now I need lots of therapy for my condition.'

A psychiatrist, John Felton, noted in a US magazine: 'Many girls build up secret love affairs with famous people. They take the pin-up poster adulation one step further and create entire lives and love affairs around them until they finally believe that they are having a relationship with that person. For someone to pretend that they are pregnant is merely taking it just one stage further. The excitement comes from the person who is smitten believing that it is their "secret" – something private and dark and mysterious. Once that illusion is shattered there is nothing left.'

Clapton still refuses to comment on the entire affair. The last word however went to Alina who said 'Dear Eric, I shall always love him ...'

The Princess and the Captain

One way or another, when it comes to affairs of the heart, the House of Windsor has had more than its fair share of anguish and pain. The Prince of Wales, who went on to become King Edward VII, scandalized society with his fling with the exquisite Lillie Langtry. A later successor to his title abandoned the throne for divorcee Wallis Simpson. In more modern times the dalliance between His Royal Highness Prince Andrew and a former soft-porn film star named Koo Stark caused more than just a little concern. But perhaps the saddest secret affair was that between Princess Margaret and Group Captain Peter Townsend; their modern-day love story rivalled anything that Shakespeare could dream up and was eventually to lead to heartbreak for them and strife within the royal family. It started as a schoolgirl crush but went on to become a deeply passionate affair which was kept secret – until a knowing glance gave them away. To this day, there are many people who think Princess Margaret was the hardest done-by royal of all.

She was just an innocent fourteen-year-old schoolgirl when she met the debonair Townsend in 1944. The twenty nine-year-old tall, war hero who had distinguished himself in the Battle of Britain, came to Buckingham Palace as an Equerry to King George VI. The appeal for Margaret was instant; Townsend was good looking, charming, distinguished – and a war hero. For a young woman, increasingly aware of her own blossoming sexuality, he was an incomparable idol. He was also unattainable – married to pretty wife called Rosemary. He was given a house in the grounds of Windsor Castle and assigned to his duties. Margaret adored him and sought him out for – allegedly – fatherly advice and friendship. There was never any question that he would be hers – yet. But in 1947 the king took Margaret and her sister, the Princess Elizabeth, on a three month tour of Southern Africa. The voyage was planned as a test of the love that Prince Philip of Greece held for Princess Elizabeth. Philip had been courting her for some while and the king thought that a long separation would test the feelings of both. Elizabeth's sadness, however, at being parted from Philip, was made up for in feelings of pure joy by Margaret – for it meant the royal party were accompanied by Group

Captain Townsend – while Rosemary stayed at home. Old newsreels of the time testify to the happiness and warmth that the seventeen-year-old Margaret radiated on the visit while she was near to the man she loved. On the visit she stayed up late into the warm African nights, listening to the cultured, witty humour and gentle views of Townsend.

For Margaret, it is almost as if she had a sixth-sense that she would one day be in his arms. She stayed away from the many suitors in society who were attracted to her, waiting for the chance to become Townsend's love. That chance occurred in 1951 when he and Rosemary parted. Their long separations due to his royal tours and other duties put a strain on the union that was too great to bear. She was unfaithful to him and in August 1951, just days after the Princess had celebrated her twenty-first birthday, Townsend told the Princess: 'The marriage is over. We married in wartime and were not right for each other.' The pair were horseriding in the grounds of Balmoral and it was there that Margaret told him for the first time of the burning passion she held for him. It was the start of the affair.

Like her predecessors within the House of Windsor, Margaret underestimated both public interest and her own family's reaction to her 'deep friendship'. The couple were once caught by the king himself as Townsend was carrying Princess Margaret up the stairs as if she were his bride and he were taking her over the threshhold! 'I told him to do it papa, I ordered him,' blurted the embarrassed Margaret who had not breathed a word of her feelings to her father. By this time Townsend was the Deputy Master of the Royal Household and as such had ample opportunity to plan his time around seeing the Princess. They arranged cosy weekends at the homes of discreet friends – a practice later adopted by Prince Andrew when he was seeing Koo Stark – and made sure never to show displays of public affection when the eyes of Britain's press were upon them. They drove away from the Palace in plain cars, Margaret often down in her seat so she would not be spotted by the curious tourists who thronged at the iron railings, craning their necks to catch a glimpse of the inhabitants. Her love for Townsend was deep, genuine – and doomed. Like all secrets, they could never keep it completely and were the subject of a vicious whispering campaign within the establishment. Townsend was accused of being a 'cradle snatcher' – Margaret guilty of foolish child-like emotions that she could neither control or understand. One of the most severe critics of the burgeoning relationship was Prince Philip, who had married Princess Elizabeth. He thought that a divorced 'employee' of the 'family firm' was not a fitting candidate to romance the Queen's sister. But Margaret was determined to share her life with Townsend – even going to see Sir Alan Lascelles, the Queen's private secretary, to enquire whether a divorce on Townsend's part – and for admitted adultery by his wife – would stand in

The early days – Group Captain Townsend and Princess Margaret.

the way of their future happiness together. Lascelles, an independent thinker, said he could see no problems as long as a 'respectable' period of time elapsed before the couple contemplated marriage. Margaret said they were thinking of a period over a year away, and he replied: 'Then I can foresee no problems.' The whole of the royal family now knew that Townsend was courting the Princess as their liaison became less secret. The British public did not. They learned about it when the couple themselves broke their cardinal rule about public displays of affection. The game was up when, shortly after the Westminster Abbey Coronation ceremony for Queen Elizabeth, Princess Margaret was observed by a Fleet Street reporter leaning forward to brush a speck of dirt from Townsend's blue RAF uniform. It was interpreted for what it was – the act of a woman in love, making sure her man looks his best. Captain Townsend's glance into her eyes gave Fleet Street sensational headlines for the next day: 'Princess Margaret's Love For RAF Hero' being one of the more reserved statements.

The couple were treated to a prime display of what Britain excels at – hypocrisy. It was 1953, the divorce rate was soaring and women were on the pathway to determining their own futures. but the establishment balked at what it felt was a constitutional crisis to rival that of the Edward and Wallis Simpson affair of the 1930s. In her role as head of state, the Queen is also the head of the Church of England, defender of the faith and the symbol of all that is sacrosanct in moral behaviour. The idea of her sister first cavorting with, and then marrying, a divorced man, was just too much to bear. Churchill was prime minister and was under great pressure to separate the couple. There were none of the kind words that the young Princess had received from Sir Alan; only a cold warning that their love could never be. Townsend was packed off to Brussels as the air attaché to the British Embassy, and Margaret was sent on a tour of Rhodesia with her mother.

The Princess, still nurturing her belief that they would be allowed to marry, called Townsend on booked international calls twice a day. The lovers plotted future trysts, secret meetings, away from both the pressure of the Palace – where Prince Philip was emerging as a major figure in mustering anti-Townsend sympathies – and the Press which had unleashed the news of the couple's love to the world. Remarkably, their romance survived. For the three years that Group Captain Townsend was posted to Brussels their affair was played out in snatched meetings and all-too-brief rendezvous at secret addresses. But shortly before her twenty-fifth birthday, Margaret was summoned by her sister, the Queen, and told that Winston Churchill had communicated to her that Parliament would never sanction a marriage to Townsend. She could renounce her royal status, and go into exile like the Duke of Windsor, but there could be no 'acceptance' into the Royal family.

In October 1955 there came the last week that the couple were to spend together. They dined at the home of friends in London and at country houses, Margaret nurturing a last ditch hope that Parliament would relent; Townsend, the wiser, elder man, knowing their affair was doomed and on its last lap. After consultations with the Archbishop of Canterbury. Margaret met with Queen Elizabeth and told her that she and Townsend had decided to call the whole thing off. On Monday 31 October, a week after crowds outside Clarence House had yelled slogans like 'marry him, marry him!', a statement from Margaret was released to the Press. The moving statement said: 'I would like it to be known that I have decided not to marry Group Captain Peter Townsend. I have been aware that subject to my renouncing my rights of succesion it might have been possible for me to contract a civil marriage. But mindful of the Church's teaching that a Christian marriage is indissoluble, and conscious of my duty to the Commonwealth, I have resolved to put these considerations before any others. I have reached the decision entirely alone, and in doing so I have been strengthened by the unfailing support and devotion of Group Captain Townsend.'

It was over. Princess Margaret went on to marry Anthony Armstrong-Jones, later Lord Snowdon. The initially blissful marriage floundered and in 1978 they were finally divorced. Friends of Margaret say that her heart had never healed from the days of that heady affair with the man who was probably her only true love.

Chapter Four

MILITARY SECRETS

The key to victory or defeat, triumph or tragedy, glory or dishonour can depend on the utmost secrecy – as was the case with Operation Overlord – the secret plan that fooled the Nazis and led to the D-Day landings. However the military mind has a darker side – a side that led to the despot generals in Argentina masterminding a secret war against their own people; and why the evil SS murdered an entire French village in a frenzied orgy of death.

Most Secret Army

The Special Air Services Regiment, or SAS, is Britain's secret army. Its officers and men are, by and large, anonymous, its numbers vague, the areas in which it moves shadowy. Part of the aura which surrounds the SAS is its strict secrecy – and that has only served to enhance its reputation as a military machine par excellence. Indeed, the reputation and rumours surrounding the regiment have become as effective as any weapon which its members include in their formidable arsenal. When the IRA gunmen holding hostages in the Balcombe Street siege in London during the 1970s heard that the SAS were on their way to reinforce police, they surrendered. When Britain entered the Falklands War men of the SAS – and its nautical equivalent the Special Boat Services – were creating havoc behind enemy lines long before the main British Task Force landed to liberate the islanders, and were dubbed 'phantom devils' by Argentine defenders. But the SAS earned a very special place in the hearts and minds of the British public when, televised for the whole world to witness, they stormed the Iranian Embassy at Princes Gate in London in May 1980, and ruthlessly eliminated five of the six terrorists holding hostages. The stark, even frightening, image of men clad from head to foot in black, with balaclavas and gas masks, abseiling from the roof of the building before bursting in through windows told the world what the British Army had long muttered in its ranks: 'Don't mess with the SAS'.

Although now widely regarded as Britain's ultimate anti-terrorist strike force, the SAS, with its motto 'Who Dares Wins', was founded in World War Two. The regiment's first commander was its creator, Lieutenant David Stirling, a veteran of the Western Desert and a man with unorthodox military ideas. In 1941 he penned a detailed memorandum about the possibility of assembling a small, lethal commando force within the British Army to work deep behind enemy lines, practising sabotage, wrecking communications and generally making a thorough nuisance of themselves to the Axis forces. He drove to the Middle East Headquarters of the British Commander in Chief, General Auchinleck, with the express purpose of seeing the chief to put his proposals to him. The British Army at the time was hard-pressed keeping Rommel from winning the desert war and was willing to listen to most suggestions. Stirling was able to present his memorandum to the General's

The SAS storming the Iranian Embassy in 1980.

Chief of Staff and three days later was given the go-ahead to launch his scheme. It was to be called L Detachment of the Special Air Services Brigade. Such a unit did not exist – but like the myths which surround the present day SAS, Auchinleck realized the immense value of propaganda and presumed that the enemy at least would think it real, conjuring up images of crack paratroops and experienced, ruthless commandos.

The success of Stirling's original band of less than 300 men in the Western Desert was real enough. Hundreds of German aircraft were destroyed on the ground by unseen attackers who melted into the desert before their explosives went off. Dozens of tanks, heavy guns, supply columns and fuel tankers were ambushed and destroyed in remote regions of the desert. Apart from an all-round skill in military tactics and weapons, the troops developed the very special skills of thriving in the harshest of climates and terrains, being able to subsist on the smallest of rations while still keeping at a mental and physical peak. That is why today for every fifteen applicants to the SAS from within the regular ranks, fourteen don't make it.

As the allied forces in 1944 and 1945 sped through occupied Europe towards Berlin, the SAS, which had quadrupled in strength, was with them

91

every hard step of the way. But by now it had started acquiring the kind of reputation which the army could only admire. In some of the most ruthless fighting in the war, savage hand-to-hand combat and behind the lines espionage, the regiment acquitted itself with remarkable results. Even the abstemious, sanctimonious Field Marshal Montgomery had to begrudgingly acknowledge the skills of the fighting men, even if their methods and their dress was somewhat unorthodox. The SAS shunned the usual discipline of the parade ground and the barrack hut – theirs was a much more specialized discipline; the need to stay one step ahead and stay alive. They evolved a system of operating which has survived to this day. The SAS men operate in pairs, linking with other pairs numbering between ten and twenty to form 'operational squads'. In the field the officers dispense with the army rule book and everyone refers to each other by their first names. Because of the almost impossible missions which the SAS set out from the start to accomplish, Stirling saw it as reasonable that previously inflexible army rules could be relaxed for fighting men who were being asked to perform beyond the range of ordinary mortals.

It was during the relentless advance through Europe that the SAS perfected its unorthodox skills. The troops became accomplished not only with every weapon in the allied arsenal, but also with those used by the enemy. They developed the skills which up until then were not required for the average British Army footslogger – to think like his enemy. As one ex-SAS man wrote: 'Forged in that iron fire assault on Nazi Germany was a unit so select, so ruthless and so damned efficient, any warlord would have sacrificed five of his best divisions for it.'

At the end of the war with the job done – the total defeat of Nazi Germany and Imperial Japan – the British government had a dilemma to solve. What to do with such an unorthodox unit. Its supporters dubbed it a remarkable band of men – its critics, a bunch of licensed brigands with little regard to legality or rules. It was of course a mixture of both. It was after the war that the SAS entered the grey, shadowy world of government plotting, intelligence and 'covert operations'. It hasn't emerged from it yet.

Initially, in 1945, the SAS was disbanded. Two years later it was re-formed as a Territorial Regiment – staffed largely by the men who fought with it during the war. By 1952 it had once again attained full regular Army status and through the 1950s until the 1980s fought long, bitter campaigns under the blanket of anonymity. A regular soldier in a regular regiment could expect glory, fanfare, a mention in his local paper and respect from the community for his heroism. The SAS man can expect only total secrecy. It is part and parcel of the job. What he can also expect from his government is a denial that he was ever in the place where he carried out his missions for the Crown.

The story of the SAS after the end of World War Two is a chronicle of the downfall of Britain as a great Imperial power. The British Empire was fragmenting at an alarming rate – troops like the SAS were over the Empire to fight against the 'terrorists' in these ugly little conflicts. In Malaya, Oman, Borneo, the Radfan, Aden and the Yemen, the SAS fought its special wars behind the lines. In Malaya, for instance, the guerrilla leaders believed they were safe in their deep jungle hideouts. Getting through the nightmarish jungles in the hope of springing a surprise attack was a naïve hope. The guerrillas killed more British troops hoping to spring surprise attacks than vice versa. To combat the enemy in his lair the SAS devised a tough paratroop training operation to land men in the heart of their territory. The only way this could be accomplished was for the paratroopers to jump straight into the treetops, snagging the parachute canopy on the high branches. Then the soldier could lower himself down on ropes to the ground below. The SAS roll of honour at Hereford, the Regimental HQ, testifies to many men who died while trying to perfect this almost suicidal method of getting to a war zone.

Successive British governments knew that the Empire's end was a foregone conclusion – often they just wanted the withdrawal from their overseas possessions to be as smooth as possible in the face of ruthless guerrillas and terror groups. In Yemen, for example, from 1963 until 1967, the SAS were there trying to aid the pro-British royalists in their fight with the republicans, who received the backing of the strong Egyptian army. It served British interests perfectly to have a royalist regime in power – it did not serve British interests to have it known that the SAS was carrying out covert missions there. Whitehall said that the Britons in action there were mercenaries. They were not – they were SAS regulars learning the ultimate lesson of 'dirty little wars' post-1945: deniability.

The system of recruitment into the SAS today allows the government to still exercise that same level of deniability when it comes to the regiment. Because the SAS is made up of hand-picked volunteers from other regiments – who often return to their 'home' units after a term with the SAS – it is easy for the government to juggle statistics and paperwork to deny the involvement of an SAS team. The 'operatives' could be sent back to their 'home' units within hours of completing a mission and then the government is able to say conclusively: there are no SAS men involved. It is effective and plunges the fighting force further from the military into the secret service. Nowhere has this been more apparent than in Northern Ireland where, for the past twenty years, Britain has been fighting a well-equipped Irish Republican Army with high losses on both sides. The SAS role in Ulster has, and continues to be, a controversial one.

Its first 'denied' operation came in 1969 and was mounted against loyalist fanatics who were smuggling weapons through the Irish Republic to the North. News leaked of SAS involvement and Prime Minister Harold Wilson denied their presence. Nearly twenty years of informed leaks to the press show that the SAS were there, but were attached to other British Army units. The Prime Minister did not lie. He just didn't expand on the quirky ways of covert operations and the need for secrecy.

It was three years after the episode in Ulster that marked a watershed in the future role for the SAS. World leaders saw the writing on the wall – that terrorism was going to be a major, ruthless factor in world power-plays. Would governments have the adequate response to it?

After the massacre of innocent Israeli athletes by terrorists at the Olympic games in Munich the SAS were specifically entrusted with the role of terrorism for the Realm. It could and would be called upon at any time to venture where others had failed and be called upon to win. In 1976 it went back, officially, to Ulster, where in the killing ground of Armagh – 'bandit country' – IRA units had succeeded in wiping out many British soldiers. After five months of 'covert' operations, eleven IRA leaders were dead, in hiding or in jail. The reputation of the SAS was only further enhanced.

Ever since, where there has been trouble, the SAS have not been very far behind. In 1973, when it was feared the liner QE2 was sabotaged with time bombs, the SAS dramatically dropped from helicopters into the ocean to board her; when South Moluccan terrorists seized a train in Holland in 1977, the SAS sent in a team to aid the Dutch forces.

In October of that year Captain Alistair Morrison and Sergeant Barry Davies flew from Britain to lead the crack German anti-terror squad GSG9 in storming a hijacked Lufthansa jet at Mogadishu in Somalia. All hostages were rescued unharmed. In 1980 there came the classic rescue of the hostages from the Iranian Embassy siege, with the loss of just one hostage in a brilliant attack which proved their expertise to the world. In 1982 they were in the thick of covert operations in the Falklands War. In 1984 they were on round-the-clock standby to deal with the Libyan Embassy siege if negotiations were to collapse. In 1988 an SAS squad killed three IRA members, who were on a reconnaisance mission in Gibraltar, plotting a bombing. That operation caused widespread anger from the Republicans in Northern Ireland and led to cries of 'state murder' from IRA sympathizers. But an inquest in September ruled that it was a lawful killing.

Police and military chiefs the length and breadth of Britain, and many from around the world, have been to secret meetings at building sites and dockyards to watch the SAS teams storm everything from a house to a liner. The SAS have developed plans for storming every type of civilian aircraft at every airport in Britain, every nuclear power plant and most high-ranking government offices. Still shrouded in secrecy, the government intends for them to stay that way, and will not publish rolls of officers' names in the Official Army List or release details of their deployment wherever it may be.

After the 1980 Iranian Embassy siege, the SAS men were driven at high speed to Chelsea Barracks in London where their commanding officer Captain Mike Rose made a speech that is now part of regimental history. He produced a pack of cards and told the men who had just made history: 'Gentlemen, this is a big boys' game. The number of cards are the ordinary people, simply wanting to go about their lives in peace. This card is the Knave – the terrorist. This card is the Queen – the one we answer to.

'And this card is the Joker – that's you lot, the wild card the Knave always has to worry about.'

The Odessa

They were destined to be the vanguard of the Thousand Year Reich – the racially pure warriors guarding the Aryan flame as it scorched the world under the doctrine of Nazism. They were members of the SS, the *Schutzstaffeln,* or Protection Squad, formed initially as a praetorian Guard for the Fuehrer, who later became the overseers and organizers of his totalitarian regime. From the concentration camps to the death squads roaming Eastern Europe and Russia, from internal security to the Gestapo, from the Reichsbank to the arts ministry, the grip of the SS was total. By the beginning of war in 1939 it had truly become what Heinrich Himmler had boasted it would – 'a state within a state'.

Apart from a few brilliant tacticians in the fighting arm of the organization, the Waffen SS, the SS was largely made up of Nazi sycophants, sadists, perverts, racial bigots and social misfits. For the appalling crimes it was to carry out, it is no wonder that the bulk of the SS was composed of men without compassion or conscience. The fabric which bound this motley crew together was the unswerving belief in Adolf Hitler and his racial doctrines

95

Simon Weisenthal – the famous Nazi hunter.

which preached world conquest and the destruction of 'lesser' peoples.

When the going was good for SS men, it was very good. Concentration camp guards were given extra rations, the killers belonging to the 'Action Squads' on the Eastern Front had unlimited alchohol and cigarettes, the men who oversaw them enjoyed the patronage of Hitler and the highest ranking members of the Nazi Party. They were the planners and the perpetrators of the foulest crimes in history – and had the war ended differently, they would have been greatly rewarded by the Reich. Instead, when the good times ended with the collapse of Germany, the SS scuttled like rats from the Fatherland – thanks to the help of one of the most secretive organizations in the world, which still exists to this day – the ODESSA.

The organisation does not take its name from the Russian city. It is an acronym for Organisation der Ehemalige SS Angehoriger – the Organization of Former Members of the SS. But this was no old comrades club. It existed for one purpose only – to get SS men out of Germany – preferably with as much money as possible – when the allies came to exact justice from the Nazi regime and its servants. Its tentacles are spread far and wide in the world, its funds nestling in secret bank accounts beneath the cobbled streets of Zurich and Geneva. Formed by SS members when the tide of war began turning and the enormity of their crimes was being discovered, the SS looked to itself and supporters to save its skin – knowing that Allied scaffolds were the only thing that could be expected after the Holocaust and the ill treatment of civilians in every part of Nazi-dominated territories.

The organization first came to the attention of allied intelligence agencies in 1949. As cries for justice against the SS members echoed throughout the world, a disturbing pattern emerged in their disappearances. They did not just vanish haphazardly from allied detention camps or from under the noses of the very people they terrorized. Rather their journeys into obscurity were well oiled, paid for with huge amounts of cash which furnished their fake papers and new lives. In a bitter twist of irony, the very bankers who withheld information from the Nazis about the funds of Jewish clients when the war started became their salvation at its end. The watchword for Swiss banks is secrecy, and the Jews – and the Nazis – were no exception. Because the war signalled the start of the biggest organized plundering expedition in history, the money to finance a covert organization intent on saving SS members was piled up over nearly six years. Much of it found its way into a reserve bank owned and operated by the *Sicherheitsdienst*, the security arm of the SS, known by its initials SD. From looted art, to gold, silver, diamonds, cash – down to the spectacles stolen from concentration camp victims – the SD deposited billions of pounds worth of loot into the banks of Zurich and Geneva. It was not in marks either, which the ODESSA organizers knew would be worthless when the war was over; the deposits made under false names and companies were in gold and the hard currencies of the allies – dollars and pounds.

But not all the ill-gotten gains were stored in Swiss banks. Billions and billions of marks' worth of gold, silver, tapestries, antiquities, art, bonds and other negotiable artefacts were siphoned off by the SD bankers. The loot was stored in huge salt mines in upper Austria and in caves in the Italian Dolomite mountains. It was this personal fortune which paid for the ODESSA to start operations at the war's close.

Experts calculate that up to £70 billion worth of the loot stolen in history's biggest robbery is still missing. It now resides with the inscrutable men who watch over the vaults of Swiss banks, and also in South American accounts and certain Arab banks. It has all been 'laundered' and is untraceable to the men who stole it. Its probable use in the forty three years since the war ended, has been to grease the pathways to freedom of the SS killers.

One man has spent his entire postwar life in the pursuit of Nazi war criminals hiding from justice. He is Simon Wiesenthal, an Austrian Jew in Vienna who survived the death camps to pursue a lone crusade against the murderers. His intelligence network of unpaid informers around the world has led to numerous arrests of wanted Nazis. But Wiesenthal knew in the very early days after the war that a secret organization existed to keep him from them. He has won considerable victories in bringing fugitives to justice, but has never defeated the machinery which spirited them away in the first place.

His expert knowledge of the ODESSA has been gleaned from secret files kept by the intelligence agencies of the West. Many, including the CIA, have a shameful past when it comes to Nazi war criminals. For when the conflict ended, focus switched from the defeat of Nazism to the new 'cold war' which loomed against the Soviet Union. Intelligence chiefs were only too willing to trade justice for the 'special skills' of wanted Nazis in the new war against communism. One of the men they enlisted was Klaus Barbie – now serving a life sentence in France for his atrocious war crimes. Another was Otto Skorkenzy, Hitler's master commando.

Skorkenzy, however, had more than knowledge about communist agents and spy networks – he was believed to be the first operative head of the ODESSA. During the war he was a gallant soldier in the Waffen SS and pulled off a spectacular glider rescue of the Italian dictator Mussolini from a mountain top. He also dressed his men up as United States soldiers during the 1944 German offensive in the Ardennes, wreaking havoc behind Allied lines.

After the war Skorkenzy traded secrets with US intelligence chiefs – except in one area: the ODESSA. Together with underlings, all using codenames, and never meeting together, they worked out the necessary details to get the

SS fugitives to safety. The favourite place to head for was South America, where the long tradition of right-wing military dictatorships favoured the refugees from a similar regime. Simon Wiesenthal says, 'In South Africa we have the Cape of Good Hope. But in South America we have the Cape of Last Hope for the Nazis. All the circumstances during and after World War Two developed it for the Nazis. About 60,000 members of the Nazi party during the 1930s live in Buenos Aires alone. All over the continent are fugitive SS men who were aided in their flight there by the ODESSA.'

Among the people who fled justice with the aid of the ODESSA were:

Alois Brunner – who designed the mobile gas-wagons to exterminate Jews at the start of the 'final solution'. He was also responsible for the deportation and deaths of 46,000 Greek Jews. Escaped to Damascus at the end of the war with ODESSA money and papers. Still at large.

Josef Mengele, notorious camp doctor of Auschwitz whose grisly experiments at the Polish death camp put him first place on Wiesenthal's most wanted list. He boasted in Buenos Aires to a German citizen several years ago that 'the comrades network', had provided him with his escape. He is widely believed now to be dead.

Joseph Schwammberger – commandant of the Polish concentration camp at Przemysl. Half a million perished under his orders. ODESSA got him to Argentina where he lives in safety.

The list goes on and on. Wiesenthal explains that it was only because of massive amounts of looting that ODESSA was able to accumulate the funds to bribe corrupt officials in the countries where the Nazis sought sanctuary.

Government agencies do not now actively pursue the old, grey men who oversaw Hitler's monstrous plan and did his bidding. Except for Israel, which is always keen to get its hands on the people who tried to exterminate the Jews, most countries are only spurred to action after repeated requests or if the media spotlight falls on them. The ODESSA has managed to keep its secrets over the years because its bank accounts are known only to a few high-ranking members. Those leaders in turn operate in small cells who do not know their counterparts. The cell system, favoured by terror groups such as the IRA, allows for people to be arrested or assassinated without the network being betrayed.

But there is not much chance of that now. Because of advancing years the ODESSA is a now dying organization. But whether or not its captured loot will be passed on to the sons of the fathers is something which Nazi hunter Simon Wiesenthal, and others who retain a conscience concerning those dark war years, want answered.

Oradour-sur-Glane

It was a hot Saturday afternoon in the sleepy town of Oradour-sur-Glane on 10 June 1944 – a town which not only the war, but time itself seemed to have passed by. Four days previously the allied armies had landed at Normandy and were fighting their way forward across Europe in the slow, bloody battle to liberate the conquered lands. True, there was excited chatter in Oradour's little café that afternoon, about the progress of the armies, the progress of their crops, and the summer fête planned for the following month. This small community of less than 700 people had toiled in their little village in the same quiet way that their forefathers had done for 800 years, and the horrors of modern warfare and the brutality of Nazism had, thankfully, passed them by.

In that long hot afternoon war and death came to Oradour. In an afternoon of killing that has long gone down in infamy, the people of the town were butchered in a frenzy of revenge and hatred by soldiers of the Das Reich Panzer division – a hitherto elite unit in the fighting arm of the SS that had distinguished itself on the Eastern Front in combat, but which had also undertaken brutal anti-partisan operations.

The women and children were herded into the village church, machine gunned, torn apart by hand grenades, burned in the ensuing flames which engulfed the building. Several young men in the fields who tried to bolt for it were picked off by SS sharpshooters who were arranged around the village at strategic points. As the smoke and stench of death rose in a grim pall over Oradour on that lazy summer afternoon, 642 people lay dead. Five survivors crawled from the smoking buildings where their fellow villagers had been murdered and were left to puzzle: why?

For years it has been assumed that Oradour was just another massacre, just another piece in the mosaic of appalling crimes perpetrated by the Nazis in all the places which they occupied. It was said that acts of sabotage by the Maquis – the French resistance fighters – had been stepped up in the region and the SS massacre was the ultimate warning to all would-be freedom fighters that the SS were not defeated and that similar atrocious punishments awaited anyone taking up arms against the Nazis. But recently new evidence has surfaced which suggests that the innocent folk of Oradour died because of a secret hoard of Nazi gold, plundered from the conquered territories. Was it this

Oradour-sur-Glane – a town destroyed by greed.

gold that the Das Reich commander was searching for the day he arrived in the town square? Almost certainly the answer is yes.

Major Otto Dickmann, a senior officer in the Das Reich division, was based in St Junien, not far from Oradour, where the remnants of the badly mauled Das Reich division were resting before joining up with the armies reeling back from the allied assault at Normandy. Among the vehicles in the long convoy stationed in the town was a truck which Dickmann referred to as carrying 'special merchandise'. He said it contained the division's records and order of battle, and gave strict orders to an Austrian Lieutenant, Bruno Walter, to double the guard on the truck. He knew that his superior, General Heinz Lammerding, were due into the town soon and he did not want the top brass breathing down his neck if the divisional transport were not well protected from the activities of the growing resistance menace. Since D-Day the Maquis had become more bold in their attacks – events had moved to the stage where SS men were having to put their hands into cow dung on the road to ensure that it wasn't booby trapped. St Junien was a centre of resistance and Dickmann could ill afford the 'special merchandise' coming under threat from the Maquis.

Dickmann, Lammerding and another Major, Helmut Kampfe, had entered into an unholy trinity in those last months of the war in France. They had survived the unbelievable butchery of the war on the Eastern Front and were now looking for some spoils to feather their own nests. All possesed Swiss bank accounts – all knew that unless a political solution was reached with the Western allies the military situation could only deteriorate. They, like countless other murderers among the ranks of the SS and Gestapo, were planning for a future without Adolf Hitler as their leader. But they needed money and the spoils of war seemed the best way of getting it. Dickmann authorized large-scale *ratissages* – looting of French towns under the pretext of searching for Maquis suspects, but in reality looking for gold. The trio had between them collected somewhere in the region of £6 million worth of gold at today's prices. In human terms the cost was beyond comparison – atrocity after atrocity was committed with the kind of barbarity that the Das Reich forces had perpetrated on the Eastern Front – this was a most terrible war, a war where there were no rules.

But the trio were stuck with the gold as they trundled to the battle area to support the flagging regular Wehrmacht forces. They could not ship it back to Germany – over a thousand acts of railway sabotage in the few months they had been in France made it too risky a venture. The three officers crated their booty and disguised it as divisional records. Lammerding decided to take the loot with them, at least as far as the Loire River, where he thought alternative arrangements, perhaps including the use of barges, could be made. It was a terrible worry for the SS men who were sure to be targets for the resistance and allied air strikes on their way.

British intelligence, thanks to the bravery of its network of agents in France, were aware that the greatly despised Das Reich division were in France and on the move with 300 heavy tanks, having swopped its looting and pillaging 'anti terrorist' role to head north to the Normandy battle zone. The resistance were planning receptions all along the route to make the Germans' journey as uncomfortable as possible. The British said that, unhindered, the German division could be in Normandy within three days, making a potentially significant contribution to the Axis forces holding the Allies in the narrow beachead zones. All and any harassment of the division would be invaluable.

At midnight on 9 June the special convoy containing the gold moved out of St Junien en-route for Bellac. Dickmann picked a circuitous route for he was as paranoid as everyone else of running into a Maquis ambush. A staff car preceded the truck, which was sandwiched between that and a half-track full of German soldiers. If all went well the convoy would have been in Bellac in a couple of hours. But all did not go well. A group of young resistance men on their way to another ambush dived for cover as the lights of the car came down the road. Fuelled by eager enthusiasm to do something for their country against the *Boche* they launched an ill-prepared ambush which, against all odds, paid off. The car exploded with a hand grenade through the window, the half track was racked by the searing explosions of several grenades and the soldiers who jumped from it and the truck were cut down in sten-gun fire. Only one German soldier escaped down the road.

Only one young resistance member survived. His six comrades, some as young as fifteen, were all dead, caught in the return fire and shrapnel from the explosions. The lone resistance survivor threw an extra grenade into the back of the truck, expecting to find more German corpses heaped inside. What he found were thirty little wooden boxes, each about the size of a shoebox. When he opened the lids he didn't find divisional records. He found gold, half a ton of it.

General Lammerding, holder of the Iron Cross First Class, decorated hero of the Russian Front, was in a rage that knew no bounds. By the following morning Dickmann felt his life was not worth living. The special convoy had been sabotaged and the gold was gone. On top of that Kampfe, his partner in crime and a longtime friend, had been kidnapped by Maquis and his fate was anyone's guess.

Lammerding had a problem. He was constantly being badgered by Field Marshall Gerd von Runstedt, supreme commander of the western front, to move his forces up to Normandy with all speed. But Lammerding wanted his 'pension' fund gold back – and used the kidnapping of Kampfe as the pretext for staying in the region while he tracked down the terrorists responsible. Kampfe was a high-ranking SS officer and it required investigation and, if necessary ruthless vengeance. But Lammerding only had twelve hours – twelve hours to find the gold which would guarantee him a happy retirement when the fighting was over.

Dickmann was summoned to Lammerding and told to find the gold. The finger of suspicion fell on Oradour – it was the nearest hamlet to the ambush site, just four kilometres away – Dickmann reasoned the only place where a half a ton of gold was likely to be taken. A notorious Captain Kahn, who had distinguished himself by his brutality and utter disregard for human life on the Russian front, was assigned to lead the search in Oradour. But it was likely that he was told it was a retribution raid, a *ratissage*, and not the search for half a ton of gold that was to provide a comfortable living for three senior officers after the war.

There are several theories about what happened in Oradour when Dickmann and 120 SS troopers rolled into the square. Did he mean for them all to die? The answer is almost certainly yes, but not before he had a chance to question them. The most likely scenario is that the hardened SS soldiers started shooting and began torching the buildings before Dickmann, who had travelled to the scene with French-speaking militiamen, could quiz the inhabitants. Either way it doesn't make much difference; there was no gold in Oradour. But the burned out houses, which have been left as they were at the end of that frightful day, are testimony to a frantic search which was carried out by the SS men. They rampaged through the buildings looking for any signs of half a ton of gold. There were none – for the gold was never there.

Robin Mackness, a former successful businessman who ran an investment management company in Lausanne, Switzerland, claims he knows the secret of what happened to the gold. In his book, *Oradour: Massacre and Aftermath*, he claims to have met a man called Raoul, the sole survivor of the ambush. Mackness, whose story about Oradour earned him praise from distinguished historian M. R. D. Foot, claims that he was asked, in 1982, to meet Raoul in France and move some 'black' gold – undeclared gold. It was Raoul who explained to him the secret of Oradour.

Raoul said that he was the survivor of the ambush on Dickmann's special convoy. He said he opened the crates, saw the gold, and carted it to a nearby field, all thirty boxes, and buried it using a shovel from the back of the truck. Then he spread twigs, leaves and grass over the scene and prayed that it didn't look like the ground had been too disturbed. Raoul raided the buried gold after the war and used it to start a small business, but now, as an old man, wanted to get it into a Swiss bank. As some of it was marked with the initials RB – Reichsbank – he knew he had to get the gold into Switzerland in a no-questions-asked manner.

But Mackness says the deal cost him twenty one months in prison after he was stopped by French customs officers near Lyons airport and found with 200,000 pounds worth of the gold in his car. He says he refused to reveal the identity of Raoul or where he got the gold from.

It is now over forty four years since the massacre and the town has been left just as it was when the last grenade had been thrown and the last round fired – an eternal monument to man's inhumanity to man. Lammerding is dead, Dickmann is dead, Kampfe is dead. And the people of Oradour died in the madness of a totalitarian rage for a secret they knew nothing about.

Overlord – The Great Secret

When Hitler's armies overran the West in 1940, he proved to the world the futility of static fortresses. His armoured units, backed by air support and swift moving infantry, showed the effectiveness of the new kind of warfare, the *Blitzkrieg*, or lightning war. Hitler's tanks had merely sidestepped the most costly land fortress system ever constructed – the Maginot Line, in which France had placed so much faith and tens of millions of francs. It was designed to keep the Germans from forever again breaching French Borders. It was the world's most costly flop. Hitler did not meet it head on – he went around the edge, pushing his armour through the Ardennes forest and completely outflanking the fortifications. The result was the capitulation of France in six weeks.

But although the Fuehrer demonstrated his contempt for the 'fortress mentality', he none the less, became a prisoner of it. When his armies were stretched in all parts of the world – in Africa, Russia, Italy, Greece and mainland Europe – he knew that it would only be time before the Allies launched an invasion. To repel such a force Hitler said that any such army was to be 'destroyed on the beaches'. And to do it, the man who showed such contempt for concrete and steel became the greatest fortress builder in history with the construction of the Atlantic Wall in France.

Entire battalions of conscripts and slave labourers were entrusted with the task of turning the French coastline into an impregnable line impossible to be breached. From the Pas-de-Calais, along the Normandy and Brittany coastlines, down the Atlantic seaboard beyond Bordeaux, and into the Bay of Biscay, the coastline was transformed into a giant pillbox, the beaches littered with mines and gruesome obstacles intended to disembowel landing craft as they raced for the beaches. Stretching northwards from France, through Belgium and Holland, through Denmark and Norway, the line zig-zagged upwards – although terrain there did not favour an invasion force.

The German General Staff knew that in order for an invasion to be successful there would have to be a) complete air superiority on the part of the invader, and b) harbour facilities to re-supply the armies at a rate quicker than the Germans could re-inforce the beachheads. If one or both criteria failed,

105

then Hitler's directive would be true and they would indeed die in their thousands on the beaches. As an invasion had to be launched from England, the General Staff calculated problems like flying time for fighters and bombers to protect the beachheads, winds, weather, favourable harbour areas, the shortest sea–distance and supply routes. Everything centred, including intelligence reports, on the Pas-de-Calais. Not only was it the nearest 'heavy-duty' port to mainland Britain, the beaches in place were flat and the tides favourable. For four years, Hitler – despite warnings in his own camp – unswervingly believed that the hammer blow would fall there. Just as unswervingly, he was ready to meet it. It was the great British deception – the secret of Overlord – that was to cost him the war.

Because it was the most obvious choice for an invasion, it rapidly became the most heavily defended region. Strung back from the cliffs were huge batteries, menacing coastal guns with the ability to lob shells into Dover twenty two miles away, and deep underground bunkers for troops that could withstand direct hits from 500 lb bombs. There was barely enough room for rock crabs to manoeuvre between the beach obstacles. Many of these obstacles had mines strapped to their sides for added effectiveness.

But the well protected Pas-de-Calais was not representative of the whole Atlantic Wall. Further down the coast, in the regions where Hitler said no armies could possibly contemplate landing, existed a potential Allied landing point. Down on the Normandy coastline, British planners as early as 1941 had studied maps, aerial photos – even pre-war French postcards – and they came up with a preliminary study which favoured striking where Hitler least expected it – the greatest armada in history would be unleashed after four years of planning to free Europe from the Nazi yoke. It was the biggest job in military history, and only secrecy would guarantee success. The intelligence job was to convince Hitler that Overlord would fall in the Pas-de-Calais – while in reality it would strike in Normandy. How?

It was on 12 March 1943 that British Lieutenant General Sir Frederick Morgan went to a meeting with Combined Operations Headquarters staff, the command run by Admiral Mountbatten. The Admiral himself greeted him warmly and announced to the other top brass members present that Morgan had assumed the role of Chief of Staff to the Supreme Allied Command – COSSAC for short. His brief: to plan for the Allied assault on mainland Europe. One month after the meeting General Sir Alan Brooke, Chief of the Imperial General Staff handed him his orders. 'There it is,' he said curtly. 'It won't work – but you must bloody well make it work!'

The task that Morgan faced was awesome. Not only had he to prepare the blueprints for the greatest invasion in history, he had to keep the plans secret and the Germans fooled. If at any time during the build up to D-Day the Germans switched their attention to the Normandy beaches and away from the Pas-de-Calais, the invasion would be scuppered. In the next fourteen months an inordinate amount of time, energy and resources were put into making the Germans believe that the blow would fall in the Calais region.

Up until 1943, it had been a relatively easy exercise to make German intelligence believe that the Pas-de-Calais was the invasion site. Most of the Nazi espionage network in Britain had been 'turned' shortly after the fall of France in 1940. Those agents who were not executed, fed a continuous stream of disinformation to their spymasters in Berlin. Only after the war's turning point – the utter defeat of the Sixth Army at Stalingrad and the reversal of fortunes on the Eastern Front – did the spectre of a second front loom large over Hitler and his generals. It was vital that new German agents, undiscovered by MI5, were fooled and fooled completely, to keep Hitler from embarking on a massive build-up of defences in the Normandy region.

But by late 1943, the build-up in Britain prior to invasion was proceeding at an almost unmanageable rate. Some two million men of an army, destined to swell to three and a half million were crammed into makeshift camps. The roads and railways systems creaked under the strain of millions of tons of supplies: tanks, heavy guns, aircraft, hundreds upon hundreds of thousands of tons of shells and bombs, millions of gallons of petrol and aviation fuel, the massive 'Mulberry' floating harbours that were being built at British ports ready to be towed to Normandy – each the size of a six storey building – and many other supplies of clothing, food and heavy machinery. General Eisenhower remarked: 'It was claimed that only the great number of barrage balloons floating constantly in British skies kept the islands from sinking under the seas.'

The problem confronting British intelligence was in convincing their opposite numbers that all these were headed for the Pas-de-Calais. Winston Churchill, Britain's wartime leader, well understood the need for deception. He created a central agency, the London Controlling Section, headed by two Englishmen, Colonel John Bevan and Lieutenant Colonel Sir Ronald Wingate, who were entrusted with fooling the Germans.

At first their campaign of disinformation was pretty standard – culminating in a bold plan called Operation Fortitude which must take much of the credit for making D-Day the success it was. It started with thousands of leaked intelligence messages, filtered through Allied-run spy networks, sloppily concealed 'secret' transmissions to Resistance groups in occupied territories, and calculated indiscretions. The Abwehr, Germany's intelligence agency, began collating report after report which signified that the Fuehrer was right – that the blow would fall in the North in the Pas-de-Calais. Espionage acts, too, were carried out all over occupied Europe, masterminded by LCS, and carried out with the aid of Britain's wartime dirty tricks brigade, the Special Operations Executive. The acts of sabotage had no strategic value for Overload – but they kept the Germans guessing and their reserves, particularly their elite Panzer divisions, dispersed over a wide area.

LCS mapped out six principal deception plans, thirty six subordinate ones and many other related strategies. The purpose of Operation Fortitude was to pin down in occupied Europe – away from the invasion zone – some ninety three German divisions. One part of the plan aimed – and succeeded – in bottling up twenty seven German divisions in Scandinavia! By creating a fictitious Fourth Army in Britain – with its command centre in the bowels of Edinburgh Castle – the German High Command was duped into thinking a heavy diversionary assault would fall on Norway. The German intelligence services were flooded with fake messages – one of them being a request from the non-existent 80th Division to Corps Headquarters for the delivery of 1,800 pairs of ski-bindings! Another message transmitted with the express purpose of being intercepted asked for woollen underwear and guides on how to scale sheer rock faces.

Still the deception went on. In neutral European capitals – hotbeds of spying for both sides throughout the war – British agents went around buying up every available Michelin map of the Pas-de-Calais region. Another masterstroke of the subversive war was the Two Generals broadcasts. The broadcasts had started shortly after 1942 and were allegedly the careless conversations of two disillusioned Germany Army officers who spoke to each other on short-wave radios about the state of the war. Germans who listened to the glum, despondent chatter of the men were suprised that there were not more careful or they would be caught. In fact the officers were German speaking actors transmitting from England in a carefully contrived plot to lower morale. In their weekly chats to each other in 1944 they dropped nuggets of disinformation about D-Day – and how they had heard that the invasion was set for Calais.

Perhaps the most brilliant stroke of all was FUSAG – The First US Army Group which was created on paper only. While Montgomery assembled his mammoth 21st Army Group in south-west England ready for the invasion, FUSAG became an army of papier-mache huts, inflatable rubber tanks, cardboard cutout camps, plywood planes and fake ammunition dumps. Fake landing craft made at the Shepperton film studios were moored on the Thames and Brtiain's leading architect, Sir Basil Spence, a professor of architecture at the Royal Academy, designed and constructed an enormous fake oil dock occupying three square miles of the shore at Dover. All of this massive fake army was in the south-east of England and was allegedly under the command of the fearsome US General George S. Patton. The German High Command was so taken in by the nonexistent Army, that they listed it in their documents of British Order of Battle.

The deception paid off – right up until the 11th hour when the strange sixth sense that had made Hitler master of Europe visited him again. In mid April Allied air-reconnaisance photographs showed a military build-up in the Normandy region, coupled with anti-glider obstacles dug into fields earmarked for Allied airborne assault. LCS was frantic that the plan had been discovered – especially when they learned that Russian-front hardened Panzer divisions were lurking in the region. But it seems to have been Hitler's intuition, nothing more, and although Normandy would be a tougher nut to crack than before, the bulk of the German forces remained thinly spread throughout the occupied lands.

By May the greatest task force the world had ever know waited for the orders to attack. A shortage of landing craft put the invasion off until June. Secrecy was at its most critical stage. One careless security lapse could mean years more of war. COSSAC had by this time given way to SHAEF – the Supreme Headquarters Allied Expeditionary Force, led by Eisenhower. A ten mile zone around all coastal areas where the invasion forces were mustered was designated out of bounds to civilians. The British government took the unprecendented step of restricting the diplomatic privileges of all countries, forbidding diplomats and their couriers from entering Britain and censoring previously sacrosant diplomatic mail. On 25 May transatlantic cable and wireless facilities for American servicemen were withdrawn. A security blanket draped over embattled Britain.

Three weeks before Overlord, Churchill met his commanders. He was told that the great deceit had worked. Germany believed that the invasion, led by the fake FUSAG army, would strike in Northern France.

They met again in June after agonizing deliberations over the foul weather. On Monday 5 June there was talk of disembarking the men from their assault craft and of postponing the invasion until it cleared. But the die was cast by the commanders. 'We go' said Eisenhower.

On 5 June 1944 the armada set sail for the beaches between Cherbourg and Le Havre. Around 5,000 ships, 11,000 planes, and the first waves of three and a half million men plunged through the black night on their mission to liberate Europe. By dawn the next morning the battleships began their bombardment of the coastal positions, thousands of airborne troops dropped behind enemy lines and the infantry were fighting their way up the beaches. Hitler's massive reserves were stirring themselves like a lizard waking up in the sun. But by then it was too late – the Allies were on the road to victory.

The Disappeared

It was given a clinical name. Like Adolf Hitler who called the extermination of European Jewry the 'Final Solution', so the military dictatorship of Argentina which embarked on one of the modern world's biggest witch-hunts did not call it murder, instead they dubbed it 'The Process of National Reorganization'. Whatever the name, humanity in Argentina ceased to exist for millions of citizens between the years 1976 and 1983. Under great secrecy and shielding behind the apparatus of the state, death squads murdered some 11,000 people, now known as The Disappeared. Two million more fled the persecution, hundreds of babies born to The Disappeared while they were being 'processed' by the military junta's servants were sold, bartered or murdered. Of the 11,000 who were butchered, experts now concur that only a handful were the left-wing terrorists who the dictatorship sought to eradicate 'root and branch'. The Process of National Reorganization, like most witch-hunts, took on a momentum all of its own. What happened in the South American nation between those years was the nearest parallel to the years of the Holocaust in the post-war world; a secret plot to eradicate all opposition, the full horror of which was only revealed after Argentina's military defeat in the Falklands War of 1982.

The military has had a long and ignoble history of meddling in the affairs of civilian governments in South America. In Argentina, it began in 1930 and continued until 1976, with the overthrow of Isabelita Peron; there had been no less than six coups and twenty-one years of military dictatorship. No civilian government had lasted its full term, save for that of Juan Peron's first period of office. On 23 March 1976, tanks rolled out on to the streets of the capital Buenos Aires and stationed themselves at the city's vital crossroads and bridges. General Jourge Videla, head of the army, proclaimed a new military junta to oust Isabelita Peron, citing the chronic inflation and massive unemployment as the reason for their intervention. Indeed, the former nightclub dancer Isabelita headed a government which saw inflation in the first quarter of 1976 run at a staggering 800 per-cent; a faster increase than the years of money-madness in post-war Germany in 1921-22. Not only did Videla pledge a re-think on policies, he promised to curb the left-wing violence that had been part of Argentine life since 1966.

The Mothers' Protest in the Plaza de Mayo.

Leftist guerrillas had been rampant in the country – kidnapping wealthy industrialists, murdering policemen, sabotaging military installations. To the military big three – Videla, and the heads of the Navy and Air Force – the country was on an inexorable slide into anarchy. The ERP, the Ejercito Revolucionario del Pueblo, the People's Revolutionary Army, and the Montoneros were the two left-wing groups that plunged Argentina into crisis. Had they not created the climate of lawlessness and terror which resulted in thousands of deaths, maybe the military would have stayed in its barracks and on field exercises. Certainly their refusal to recognize the elected government of Hector Campora – elected freely and fairly in 1973 – to continue their bloody revolutionary war was a major factor which prompted the nightmare military response. Videla and his generals were under no illusions what that response would be. It would be total war – carried out not only against the known guerrillas, but against those that they deemed may have a tendency for left-wing action or sympathies. In the dirty war that Videla was about to unleash, thought, association or sympathy with any policy other than that dictated by the junta were crimes punishable under the

111

'Process of National Reorganization'.

After the coup, greeted with calm by most people, sickened of both inflation and the guerrilla war, and with positive joy among the wealthy business community, Videla's government issued a statement to the world pledging full respect for 'law, human dignity, and Argentina's international obligations ... the fundamental objective will be to ensure essential values in leadership, assuring the full development of the country's natural and human potential.' Secretly, the machinery of terror was being assembled. Argentina's military, particularly her officers had long been instilled with a sense of divine purpose – that theirs was a noble cause, protecting Argentina and her strategic place in the world among the great nations, as a bulwark against communism. Now they were told that the final conflict had arrived; that indeed their Third World War against the heretics of Marxism had come.

By 1976, the Argentine officer corps was a different body to the generations that had preceded it. Over 600 Argentine officers had attended a course, started by the John F. Kennedy administration, at the US Army School of the Americans, based in Panama. Although intended by a democratic nation to show South American nations how to defeat communist revolution and maintain the support of the populace, the school taught many gruesome subjects – not the least of them torture. This, coupled with the ceaseless indoctrination in their home country served to equip the Argentinian officers for a covert war against the masses.

Survivors of the terror, those who implemented it and those who were on the receiving end, are among those who testified that the strategy for the 'Process' was worked out at a top secret meeting hosted by Videla in 1975. Accounts, naturally, are sketchy, because no documents testifying to their evil scheme have surfaced. What seems to have happened is this: Videla requested detailed methods of dealing with the guerrillas drawn up by the intelligence chiefs of the three services. Roberto Viola, the general who became Videla's brief successor before General Galtieri in 1981 was there. So were high-ranking intelligence chieftans of the Navy and Air Force. Viola is reported to have argued against the policy which, Videla said, meant the complete and total disappearance of the regime's critics. The state was to act as judge, jury and executioner.

A vivid foretaste of what lay in wait for the people of Argentina was delivered next month, October 1975, when Videla gave a speech in Montevideo, capital of neighbouring Uruguay. He said: 'In order to guarantee the security of the state, all the necessary people will die. A subversive is anyone who opposes the Argentine way of life.'

Only after Britain's victory in the Falklands and the downfall of the dictatorship in Argentina did the misery and wholesale suffering of those years come to light. The terror was directed by the Ministry of the Interior where a master list of those who vanished was said to be kept. But in reality the mayhem loosed on the unfortunate population had little direction or guidance. Each military branch had its own intelligence service masterminding kidnappings, torture and executions. On top of those were the actions of the National Gendarmerie and the police. In addition several government ministries, even the national oil company, held lists of suspects and had security agencies operating for them. The separate arms of state, all vying for the dubious glory of arresting more subversives, caging more innocents, torturing more women, created a system of total mayhem. The kidnappings were done by men dressed in plain clothes. The unfortunate relatives were met with a stone-wall at police stations and government offices. 'How can we tell you what happened, when we have no record of arrest? It must be the terrorists responsible.' It was the stock answer repeated over 11,000 times.

Green Ford Falcon cars became the symbol of the terror, in much the same way as Madame Guillotine had been in the French Revolution two centuries earlier. The four-door cars were packed with men from the *patotas*, the arresting squads. The Falcons cruised down streets keeping a watch for suspects who were then bundled into the boot and oblivion. The *patotas* were heavily armed with pistols and sub-machine guns and used violence at the slightest sign of a struggle during an abduction.

The Disappeared were taken to torture and interrogation centres all over Argentina – places with innocuous sounding names like the Navy Mechanics School on the outskirts of Buenos Aires. A name resonant of research and study; in reality it was a human abbatoir where people were beaten, electrocuted, maimed and finally 'processed' so they were no longer a threat to the right-wing regime which ruled Argentina. The military had long ago decided that ordinary prisons were no solution to terrorism and so set up these sinister, secret detention and torture centres all over the country.

At the Navy Mechanics School was one Lieutenant Alfredo Astiz, a prominent torturer who was responsible for the death of two French nuns among the myriad hordes caught up in the process. Astiz was captured during the Falklands War and spent a short time in Britain before he was packaged back off to Argentina where he now lives freely, unlike so many of his tragic victims.

The military disposed of the bodies of their victims in two ways – in the 'doorless flights' over remote stretches of the River Plate, or by the 'NN' method. The doorless flights were named after the aircraft and helicopters whose doors were either removed or constantly open, allowing the military to dump bodies in remote regions and into the river. As many as 5,000 victims were disposed of in this way.

The NN's were the victims with no-name. Buried in their thousands all over Argentina, the bodies still continue to be found to this day.

Such wholesale disappearances, of everyone from students, university professors, nuns, priests, to clerks and business executives, could not fail to arouse the interest of the world humanity watchdog. Amnesty International. Amnesty first visited Argentina before the end of 1976 and compiled a chilling dossier of life in the state prisons where women told of sexual abuse, torture and humiliation. The Amnesty investigators were shocked – but they hadn't seen all. They still had no knowledge of the secret detention centres which made the prisons look like citadels of decency.

Allen 'Tex' Harris was one of the heroes of the dirty war who saw the Argentinian situation for what it was and relayed it in detail to the authorities in Washington. As a first secretary as the US embassy in Buenos Aires he was entrusted with the task of monitoring human rights violations. He and his assistants chronicled no fewer than 15,000 cases which were sent to the Jimmy Carter administration in Washington. He discovered that it was not a campaign aimed at terror groups and fought between terror groups, but a systematic war against the people of Argentina. He said: 'They killed some real terrorists in shoot-outs early on, sure enough, and they captured some too. But the great majority of the ones they captured were just wine-and-coffee subversives – kids who sat in cafés talking about socialist ideals and how the country should be changed.

'There was a guy from Army intelligence who told me in person that the real tragedy of their operations was that half the people eliminated were innocent even by their own criteria. But it was easier to kill them because it was less risky and less compromising than going through the legal procedures. Easier to handcuff them to a lamppost and just shoot them.'

But governments had little to congratulate themselves on as the toll of human rights abuses continued to mount. The United States made noises on rights abuses and sought guarantees on improvements – but the thinking in Washington was undeniably that a right-wing regime was infinitely preferable to a left-wing one. The Soviet Union, heavily reliant on the United States for grain, did not want to antagonize a potentially major supplier in case Washington turned unfriendly. Britain played a cool behind-the-scenes game with the Argentine junta over the relatively few British people, or those of British descent, who had vanished.

Two things blew apart the secrecy, and it is debatable which was the more powerful. One was the Falklands War in 1982, the other the Mothers of the Plaza de Mayo.

The tactic of making people vanish without trace had proved its effectiveness as early as 1977, one year after the junta took power. There were no martyrs to the cause – indeed, there were no state records of prisoners. There were no demonstrations in the West about Argentina as there had been about Chile and no government had severed diplomatic ties with Videla. But on the afternoon of Saturday 13 April 1977, a small demonstration took place which would become a milestone in Argentine history. Fourteen women, who had lost sons, husbands, daughters, brothers and sisters in the terror staged a solemn walk in the Plaza de Mayo outside the Casa Rosada, the pink palace residence of Argentina's rulers. The walk was formed by Hebe Bonafini and Adela Antokaletz, two women who had both lost loved ones: Mrs Bonafini, her two sons and a daughter-in-law; Mrs Antokaletz her son. The movement grew from a few women pronounced as 'mad' by the Generals, to dozens, who paraded every week despite clubbings, tear gassings and arrests. In the end the military left them alone – the Mothers had won the right to the Plaza and the world bore witness to their silent, noble stand.

In the end, the military became as inept at running the country as the civilians they overthrew. In 1982, in a mad venture, as the economy reeled from the years of murder instead of economic planning, they launched an attack on the Falkland Islands off the southern tip of Argentina. Long a symbol of national pride, *Las Malvinas* were in the hands of the junta for a matter of weeks before a well-trained force from Britain resoundingly defeated them and reclaimed the windswept islands for the Realm. It signalled the total collapse of the junta.

In Argentina in December the following year, Raul Alfonsin came to power as a democratically elected president and the full horror of those years came to light. The graves were discovered the length and breadth of the enormous land, torturers stepped up to confess their crimes and the killers wrung their hands and said they were doing their duty.

So far several hundred Argentine military officers have been sentenced for their crimes, and several hundred more face court hearings. The Mothers of the Plaza de Mayo still tread their weary way in front of the Casa Rosada; those who lost loved ones still wonder how they ever let it happen. But in a volatile land, where the military is never far away from heading for parliament, many fear that justice will stop far short of what they deserve.

'They did it in secret and in silence,' said Mrs Bonafini, who still cries at the thought of the loved ones she lost and has never seen again. 'The world could not imagine our suffering. Let it serve as a warning to other countries not to put faith in military men like we did in Argentina.'

The Manhattan Project

Over forty years have elapsed since the vision of a mushroom cloud of smoke rising over a Japanese city called Hiroshima burned itself forever on the human consciousness. In that split second man unleashed the forces of nature that he had learned to harness in the century's most top-secret research and as a result the nuclear age was born. After that explosion, nothing would ever be the same again. The world now lies split into two camps, each with enough nuclear hardware to make the Hiroshima bomb look like a firecracker. The United States developed the bomb under conditions of amazing secrecy in a research programme called The Manhattan Project. Led by brilliant phycisist Dr Robert Oppenheimer, the Americans were engaged in a frantic race against time – for in a world at war, Nazi Germany was also engaged in its own research to split the atom. Although behind the US effort, the fact that Hitler's scientists were engaged in research made President Franklin Roosevelt aware that, no matter what the cost, the free world had to achieve the first atom bomb and thereby completely ensure its supremacy over the forces of Germany and Japan.

It was the rise of Nazism and the war which caused groups of European scientists, many of them Jewish, to flee to the United States. As early as 1933 these brilliant men and women warned that Nazi scientists had been given huge budget increases to pursue the dream of a controlled nuclear reaction – in effect, a bomb of awesome power. In 1938 US intelligence learned that outside Berlin, in a closely guarded laboratory, the Germans had succeeded in splitting a single atom. They had not harnessed its energy, but they were on the way. It was enough to spur the most eminent phycisist of this, or any age, to write to the President of the United States urging him to push for nuclear research – and quickly.

Dr Albert Einstein, father of the theory of relativity, was one of those banished from Nazi Germany because he was a Jew. He wrote an impassioned letter to Roosevelt, who was still struggling to rebuild the US economy from the days of the great depression which had devastated the United States. The plea from such an eminent scientist shocked Roosevelt and moved him to

Hiroshima – devastated by the atomic bomb.

order research effort on the bomb. Even though the United States was neutral in the war until 1941, Roosevelt and his advisers were of the opinion that the prize of nuclear supremacy should belong to the mightiest industrial nation.

Since the turn of the century scientists had known that the element uranium naturally disintegrated by emitting alpha particles containing neutrons and protons – a process yielding a spectacular million times more energy per atom than ordinary fire. The only problem was – the process took millions of years as part of the natural evolutionary process of earth. What if that process could be speeded up, harnessed – and unleashed? The prospect for scientists was breathtaking and frightening.

Enrico Fermi, an Italian scientist who came to the United States in 1938 from Mussolini's Italy, was awarded the 1938 Nobel Prize for his research into atomic energy and shortly afterwards came to America to take up a teaching post at the University of Columbia. Fermi learned there of the German experiment in Berlin. Together with several eminent scientists from around the world, he began his first experiments into nuclear fission.

Fermi was one of the first scientists to throw a veil of secrecy around the research. In the early days it was an academic project, not sanctioned by the

117

government or military. He had to warn his colleagues – long used to trading information with other scientists and boasting of their progress in scientific journals – to remain silent. The military were later to complain that the security in those early days was 'leaking like a sieve'.

Before building a bomb, the scientists first had to learn how to split the atom and harness its energy. By mid-1938 Roosevelt had authorized the Manhattan Project as a government funded programme for the bomb and, realizing the need for secrecy, decreed that the separate research programmes were to be carried out at sites and locations spaced widely apart. A secret bunker complex was carved out of the Nevada desert in New Mexico, where it was ultimately hoped the bomb would be tested. The research into splitting the atom was carried out under Fermi's guidance in Chicago.

The breakthrough came on 3 December 1942, on a sports field in Chicago. Fermi assembled his research team with the device which would trigger a nuclear chain reaction; the first step to forming the 'critical mass' which becomes the nuclear explosion. The scientists had built a nuclear 'pile', a primitive nuclear reactor designed to test whether nuclear energy could be triggered in a chain reaction and harnessed for energy. The reactor took the form of a spheroid shape, packed with uranium which would be bombarded with neutrons and protons as safety rods inserted into the device were removed one by one. On hand were a 'suicide squad' of firefighters – armed with nothing more than a few buckets of water to put out Earth's first man-made nuclear fire if the chain reaction were so violent that it caught fire!

The sports field had been sealed off for three miles around by police and security agents desperate to shield the experiment that was taking place. Anyone wishing to go near the place was told that soil samples for a new government farming programme were being taken.

One by one the rods were pulled – Fermi witnessed the geiger counters monitoring the berserk levels of radiation as they pulsed through the sphere, triggering the massive chain reaction 'Throw in the safety rods' cried Fermi at the last minute before the sphere looked likely to explode in that most dangerous of nuclear accidents – meltdown. The experiment worked and Fermi celebrated man's arrival in the atomic age with a bottle of Chianti!

However, just as the Manhattan Project got under way properly in 1942 – building the bomb in the Nevada desert complex – some of the physicists engaged became worried about the nature of their tasks. They were concerned with the nuclear destruction that they might be unleashing on the world. It was a question of conscience that caused more than one scientist to leave the project – and gave a security headache to the agencies concerned with keeping secret the most important research of the war. All the scientists involved were required to sign secrecy oaths – but for good measure many were kept under the scrutiny of the military for months afterwards.

The military man in charge of the project was a bluff brigadier-general named Leslie Groves. He was a man used to giving orders and used to having them obeyed. He more than anyone impressed on the men of science the need to keep the project secret. He pointed out that one of the prizes which fell to the German war machine in 1940 during the battle of Norway was the Norsky Hydro Hydrogen Electrolysis plant, which manufacturered heavy water – the most efficient substance, say scientists, for the construction of a chain-reacting atomic pile. Although the plant was later crippled in an Allied commando raid, Groves told the scientists 'Make it quicker, without being caught, and we'll have them. Don't and they will have us.' The work progressed with everyone involved aware of the need for urgency.

The giant Du Pont company was given the government order to manufacture enough plutonium for the bomb. Government contracts everywhere for the manufacture of the weapon were disguised as something else – research into pesticides, research into solar power, research into alternative fuels. The steel delivered for some of the prototype bomb casings was marked down as steel for artillery barrels.

By 1945, a prototype had been developed and, by July, was ready for testing. In the middle of the New Mexico desert Operation Trinity, the code name for the testing, was set for the 16 July. The bomb was called Fat Boy and the site for its testing was ten miles from the Alamagordo Air Base, a complex of underground bunkers and buildings where much of the construction of the bomb had been carried out. A host of military and scientific top brass were assembled to witness the largest explosion ever made by man on Earth. At 5.30 a.m. in the cold drizzle, a ball of fire reaching 41,000 feet, 12,000 feet higher than the tallest mountain, soared above the desert. The thunder from the explosion reverberated across the open spaces, shaking the ground as if an earthquake were about to consume the earth. Oppenheimer, in that fearful moment, recited two verses from Sanskrit, the ancient language of India. One was: 'If the radiance of a thousand suns were to burst into the sky, that would be the splendour of the mighty one.' The second was: 'I am become Death, the shatterer of worlds.'

Three months before the test the most secret airfield ever constructed was built at Tinian, a Pacific island situated near Japan. The inhabitants of the island were completely isolated from the world as teams of engineers and construction workers carved out the forward atomic base from where an elite airwing, the 509th, would be based to carry out the nuclear attack on Japan. President Harry Truman had sanctioned an American nuclear assault on the Japanese mainland in an effort to save American lives as Japanese troops fought fanatically to the death in their bid to hold their ground. The 509th was formed in conditions of such secrecy that even the top ranking scientists and officers on the Manhattan Project did not know that a squadron with the sole purpose of delivering the bomb to Japan had been formed.

The secrecy surrounding the bomb and the delivery of atomic material to Tinian for final bomb assembly had tragic consequences. The cruiser Indianapolis was loaded with the radioactive cargo sailed from San Francisco to Tinian and on its return voyage was torpedoed. Because its mission was so secret the naval command did not know its exact position or whereabouts. As a result nearly 400 men died in the shark infested waters before any rescue vessels were sent to their aid. It was one of the war's prime examples where secrecy overrode every consideration – including human life.

The plane that was to carry the bomb was to be piloted by the United States' top flyer, Captain Paul Tibbets, who named the B-29 bomber the Enola Gay after his mother. On 6 August 1954 Mrs Tibbets achieved fame of a kind when the bomb was dropped on Hiroshima. In the blinding light of the nuclear explosion, equivalent of 20,000 tons of TNT, 150,000 people were incinerated, thousands more suffering the appalling burns of radiation.

The Manhattan Project was successful and Dr Robert Oppenheimer was right; he had become the shatterer of worlds.

Chapter Five

SECRETS OF HOLLYWOOD

In a place where sincerity is as real as a studio backdrop, it is no surprise that Tinsel town's residents have many secrets. Secrets like the sex life of Rock Hudson – the ultimate macho actor whose homosexuality led to his death; or the shocking secrets in film star Mary Astor's infamous diary – a work that made the *Kama Sutra* pale by comparison; and then there were the murders – who killed respected director, William Desmond Taylor?

The Double Life of Rock Hudson

The Hollywood dream factory is a remarkable thing. It can recreate the parting of the Red Sea on a studio backlot, turn a sound stage into a galactic war zone, or make Fred Astaire dance on the ceiling. But in Tinsel Town, where they hand out awards from trickery and deception, things are seldom as they appear.

So it was with Rock Hudson. For almost forty years, this master of the silver screen lived a secret, double life. In public he was the most dashing screen hero of his generation – a rugged, macho love god idolized by women and envied by men all over the world. But in private he was a far cry from the debonair lady-killer of his films. He was a homosexual, whose lusting for taboo love eventually cost him his life ... and shattered the image he had carefully cultivated throughout his career. It was a secret Rock had dearly wanted to take with him to the grave – and probably would have, had he not fallen victim to the disease society has labelled the 'gay plague'.

Even after AIDS was first diagnosed, Rock tried to continue living the lie, and swore his closest friends to secrecy. Eventually, of course, neither he nor they could remain silent, once the devastating effects of the disease became obvious. And so, just a few weeks before his death, the screen giant reluctantly admitted the secret he had kept hidden for so many years.

Back then, Rock Hudson, film star was just plain Roy Fitzgerald, Navy veteran, vacuum cleaner salesman and would-be actor. He worked hard, saving what money he could, and whenever he had a spare moment, would stand outside the gates of the movie studios, waiting to be discovered. It was a lonely time for Roy, as he recalled many years later: 'It was very difficult for me to make friends. People weren't friendly like they were in the Mid-West.'

But by the following year, the struggling actor had made some friends ... friends who would change his life forever: the gay community of nearby Long Beach. It was natural for Roy to feel at home among his own kind. Ever since his days in the Navy, he had preferred the company, and sexuality, of men. But Roy got more than sex and friendship from those he met – he also got his first break on the way to becoming an international sex symbol.

Some of his fellow gays had connections in showbusiness and, at a party in

122

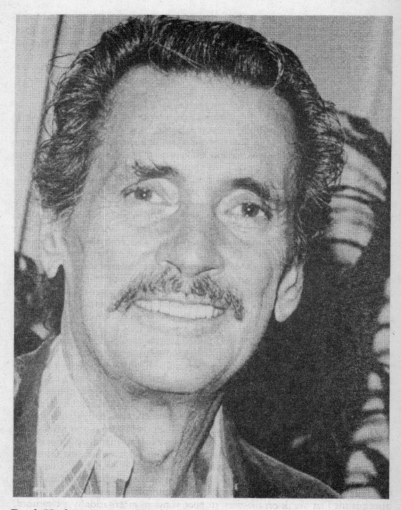

Rock Hudson at one of his last public appearances.

1948, Roy was introduced to Henry Willson, a fellow homosexual and head of talent for the David O. Selznick Studio. Willson, who could spot that elusive 'star quality' at a glance, signed Roy to a studio contract and changed his name to Rock Hudson.

It was during this time that Rock also met two fellow gays, George Nader and Mark Miller. The three would remain close friends all their lives. Mark, a one-time singer, had given up his career in order to become Nader's business manager. Nader, like Rock, was exceptionally good-looking and wanted a career in the movies. But all three knew that if he and Rock were ever going to make it, they could not allow even a hint of scandal about their sexual preferences to get into print. Rock went to some bizarre lengths. He always made sure he had two phone lines in his apartment, and his room mate was never allowed to answer Rock's, lest someone discovered that Rock was living with another man. He and George also developed code-words to talk to each other in public. 'Is he musical?' was a code for 'Is he gay?'

In 1953, Rock, who had already appeared in several films, though was not yet considered a star, met Jack Navaar, a twenty-two-year-old friend of Nader's. The two hit it off immediately and within a few weeks, the dynamic-looking couple were lovers and room mates. But Rock could never publicly show any affection for Jack, and even when his first big film, *Magnificent Obsession*, premiered the following year, he was forced to bring a script girl from the studio as his date. Jack, who arrived in a separate car, was also given a female escort. Studio bosses knew they had a potential superstar on the rise, and they didn't want the press to get a whiff of scandal. 'Universal invested a lot of money in Rock, and it was important for his image to remain that of a lady-killer', said Mamie Van Doren, a friend of Rock's.

Unfortunately for Jack, however, fame soon went to Rock's head, and the once-happy couple began to argue bitterly about anything and everything. To make matters worse, Jack couldn't even go out to dinner with his lover anymore, because *Magnificent Obsession* had made Rock a huge celebrity. Inevitably, within twelve months, the affair was over – and Hudson, his career booming, would not live with another man for a decade.

But in 1955, despite Rock's intricate precautions, the Hollywood scandal sheet *Confidential* was threatening to write an exposé on his taboo love affairs – which would destroy not only his career, but financially cripple the studio as well. To kill the story, the studio and Rock decided that he should get married, which he did on 9 November.

The hastily arranged nuptials, to his agent's secretary, Phyllis Gates, saved his career. Unfortunately for Phyllis, she was never told the marriage had been planned by the studio bosses, or that Rock was gay. Many years later, she recalled that Rock had managed to keep his homosexuality from her until

124

the very end of the relationship, which lasted almost three years.

By 1960, Rock was the world's number one box office attraction, and had just completed his first comedy, *Pillow Talk*, with Doris Day. It was about this time that he began to be driven more by sex, than his career. After all, he had now made it to the top, and all those years of self-sacrifice and self-discipline were about to be abandoned. Rock even confided to friends that he thought about having sex all the time during this period, even while driving his car or rehearsing his lines.

In the next ten years, he had numerous lovers, but still managed to keep his secret from the public, thanks to loyal friends and discreet colleagues within the industry. It was a precaution he had to take. Even a malicious gag could almost end a career, as Hudson found out in the early 1970s. A vicious hoaxster sent out invitations to gossip columnists, inviting them to the 'wedding' of Rock and good friend Jim Nabors. The tasteless prank ruined Nabors' career, whose prime-time variety series was cancelled soon after, even though he and Hudson were never more than friends.

The experience left Rock even more paranoid about his secret life, and he avoided Hollywood night life more and more. Instead, he would entertain guests at his Beverly Hills mansion, where a string of handsome young men would lie around the pool waiting to offer their services.

In 1973, Rock again took a full-time housemate and lover – Hollywood publicist Tom Clark, whom he'd met ten years earlier. Clark, a far cry from the pretty boys that had walked in and out of Hudson's bedroom over the years, would become the most important person in the actor's life. They were inseparable for many years, and spent wonderful times doing things they both loved – drinking, cooking, travelling, watching football and making love. But in Tom, Rock also found something very special. For the first time in his life, he had a man with whom he could walk down the street, take to restaurants and studio parties. Tom, you see, had become Rock's personal manager and publicist ... a legitimate connection.

'I can take him anywhere,' Rock confided to friends. 'I can even introduce him to Princess Margaret.'

In 1975, Rock turned fifty – and Tom threw him the 'prettiest party we ever had.' As the guests mingled in the party room, the hired band struck up *You Must Have Been a Beautiful Baby*. Down the staircase came the birthday boy, wearing only a nappy, as the guests whistled and cooed.

Of course, there were many other parties at Rock's mansion over the years. Once, in 1977, just before he returned home from a three-month tour, he called secretary Mark Miller and said: 'I want a beauties' party when we get home. Could you arrange it? Have a party waiting for me at the house.'

Miller obliged. He invited ten of Rock's closest friends, and fifty handsome young men! One of the guests later recalled: 'There were some of the best-looking men I'd seen in my life.'

But the pleasures of the party were short-lived. That same year, Rock hit bottom, drinking all day, worrying about his age and sliding career and even took to touring homosexual clubs in San Francisco where anything went. Ironically, it was at about this time that the AIDS virus was taking a foothold within the gay community. Rock's sex and drinking binge lasted almost four years, until, in November 1981, he was forced to undergo by-pass surgery on his heart. It was, quite literally, a sobering experience.

'He woke up from the drunkenness of the '70s,' said old friend George Nader. 'The meanness and sniping fell away, and he was returning to the Rock we had known in 1952 — a warm human being who laughed and played games.'

But he was no longer devoted to Tom Clark. In 1982, Rock began to have a lusty affair behind Tom's back with a much younger, more virile man, Marc Christian. Within a year, Tom was tossed out of the house, and Marc moved in. It was to be Rock's most passionate, and final relationship.

In 1984, Rock was invited to a White House dinner, where he gladly posed for pictures with President and Mrs Reagan. A few weeks later, the photographs arrived at his office, personally signed by the First Couple. As he and secretary Miller looked at the photos, they noticed a red sore on Rock's neck. It had been there for over a year, but it had become bigger.

Under Miller's constant nagging, Rock eventually decided to see a doctor about the sore . . . and on 5 June 1984, he received the news he had dreaded. It was AIDS. But Rock still wasn't about to let his secret out; not yet, anyway. Those few friends he did tell were sworn to secrecy, as the dying actor vainly sought a cure. Marc Christian didn't know Rock had AIDS until February 1985, even though they continued to have sex; and Linda Evans, the actress whom Rock kissed on an episode of *Dynasty* didn't know until the world did. Rock had lived a lie for so long, that he couldn't even bring himself to tell the truth to those close to him. It wasn't until the end was near, when death was certain, that he finally revealed his dreadful secret.

Fans around the world were understandably shattered, and yet they responded to his plight with sympathy and renewed curiosity about this mystery disease. Suddenly, AIDS was on the front pages of newspapers around the world; research funds were set up; the United States Congress vastly increased efforts towards finding a cure; the United Nations hosted conferences on it; everywhere, people wanted to learn more about the disease which had taken their idol.

Ironically, the secret Rock felt he could never share with the world has spurred that same world to action. Rock's defeat may become his victory.

Death of a Hollywood Director

On the morning of 2 February 1922, celebrated film director William Desmond Taylor was found lying on the floor of his Hollywood bungalow, a diamond ring on his finger, a smile on his face – and a bullet in his back.

Today, more than sixty-five years later, the identity of his murderer remains one of Hollywood's most tantalizing secrets, a 'whodunnit' in the greatest traditions of the cinema.

It had everything: sex, drugs and scandal; an evil, exploitative stage mother; a sexy young starlet; an affable, handsome director who happened to be bisexual, and a studio that was prepared to go to any lengths to cover it all up.

But what makes the Taylor case even more fascinating is that several people either saw the murderer enter or leave the house, and yet no one was ever charged with the crime! The moguls of Hollywood, it seems, had influence over more than just the movie world, and they knew a trial would only further scandalize an industry still reeling from the Fatty Arbuckle rape trials in San Francisco.

Indeed, when the police were finally called to Taylor's residence that sunny afternoon, they found no fewer than eleven of his friends and colleagues scurrying about the house in an attempt to 'sanitize' the murder scene. Studio heads were trying to erase any signs of homosexual misconduct, while comic star Mabel Normand was hunting for love letters she had written to Taylor. Sweet-faced Mary Miles Minter, the nineteen-year-old *ingénue* who also shared the director's favours, was doing likewise.

In spite of the impromptu house cleaning, however, police still discovered a hoard of scandalous material which the intruders hadn't had time to destroy.

According to accounts of the time, authorities found a stack of pornographic pictures of Taylor with various women of the stage and screen, as well as a collection of fine silk lingerie, including one rose-coloured nightie bearing the initials MMM. Police also found some of the love letters which had eluded the two actresses' frantic search.

Subsequent investigations revealed even more disconcerting facts about

127

William Desmond Taylor in army uniform.

Taylor. He was really William Deane-Tanner, a New York antiques dealer who had walked out on his wife and family fourteen years earlier, and that his mysterious butler, Sands, was really his brother. Sands, a dubious figure who had been in trouble with the law a few years earlier for passing bad cheques, vanished shortly after the murder and was never seen again.

To say Hollywood was in shock is an understatement. It was reeling, for not only was Taylor one of the most respected film-makers in the business, but he was also a social figure of some standing, and had even been the president of the Screen Directors' Guild. Further, the newspapers of the time hinted that Taylor had been the reason screenwriter Zelda Crosby, with whom he had also been intimate, committed suicide.

But there was still more scandal when it was learned that on the night of the murder, Mary Miles Minter, followed by Mabel Normand, had separate trysts with Taylor – his reputation as a Lothario was apparently well-founded.

According to a neighbour, Mrs Faith MacLean, about ten minutes after Mabel left, she heard what she described as a small explosion. She went to her door and in the shadows saw a man running from Taylor's house. The man, seeing her, hesitated, and returned to the bungalow, as if he had simply forgotten to tell the director something. His cool reaction convinced Mrs MacLean that nothing was amiss, and that the noise she'd heard had been a car backfiring.

But Mrs MacLean had indeed seen the killer, and yet her description of the suspect only deepened the mystery.

'It was dressed like a man,' she later recalled, 'but you know, funny-looking. It walked like a woman – quick little steps and short legs.'

Her description fuelled speculation that the killer may have been a woman – and indeed, just two years ago, author Sidney Kirkpatrick announced he had solved the murder and named Mary Minter's domineering mother, Charlotte Shelby, as the long-sought killer.

Kirkpatrick claimed that Mrs Shelby, an evil woman who made the young starlet's life a misery, had forbidden Mary from seeing Taylor. When she learned they were having a torrid affair behind her back, the enraged Shelby killed her daughter's lover.

Other writers and investigative reporters also suspected Shelby, but they say jealousy, and not a mother's outrage, was the motive. According to these amateur sleuths, Shelby and Taylor were also locked in a torrid relationship and she killed him when she learned he had also been bedding her daughter.

Kirkpatrick's information came from the memoirs and artefacts of the late director, King Vidor. In 1967, Vidor claimed he had finally solved the mystery of Taylor's death, and had planned to make a film based on the extraordinary case to herald his comeback to the big screen. Unfortunately for Vidor – and crime buffs everywhere – he died before he could reveal his secret. Kirkpatrick says he stumbled across what he claims to be proof that Mrs Shelby was the killer while doing research for a biography on Vidor.

However, according to other crime historians, both Kirkpatrick and his colleagues who named Shelby as the murderer, overlooked the fact that the person Mrs MacLean saw leaving the Taylor house after the shooting was the same person other witnesses said had earlier asked for directions to the director's home: And they had no doubts that person was a man.

Also, it must be remembered that Mary Minter hated her mother to her dying day, and if there was ever a hint Mrs Shelby had shot the director, the young actress would have gladly accused her publicly.

Could then, the killer have been Taylor's brother, the shadowy butler, Sands? Unfortunately, that too, appears unlikely. Given Sands' dark past, surely he would have ransacked the house for the money and jewels which lay untouched by the murderer. No, this was a crime of passion.

Maybe it was an irate husband, who had learned of Taylor's dalliance with his wife. Just one year after the murder, police had already compiled a list of 200 possible suspects! However in the end no one came to light as the culprit, as the identity of Taylor's murderer remains a mystery.

Sadly, Taylor was not the only victim of this bizarre mystery. Hollywood may have felt the wrath of an indignant public once the lurid details of the directors' secret life hit the newspapers, but it was Mabel and Mary who became the scapegoats for the powerful film moguls.

During the investigation, it became known that Mabel had a heavy cocaine habit, the kiss of death for actors back in the 1920s. The two-faced 'puritans' who ran the studios took her films off the market, forever destroying her once-brilliant comic career.

As for poor little Mary, she also became too much of an embarrassment to the movie world. At Taylor's funeral, she approached the coffin and kissed her lover's corpse full on the lips. She then caused another sensation by telling the congregation: 'He whispered something to me. It sounded like "I shall love you always, Mary."' One newspaper called it 'her greatest performance'.

That little outburst – together with the juicy details of her affair with Taylor, which by now had been blasted all over the pages of Hollywood's racy tabloids – forced Mary into a hasty retirement and a life-long battle with obesity. She died in 1984.

Fatty Arbuckle - King of Comedy

Roscoe 'Fatty' Arbuckle was every child's favourite clown. Parents loved him too as the champion of good clean fun; an affable, roly-poly star of the silent screen who would do anything to make a youngster smile, whether it be by taking falls in the mud or custard pies in the face.

But unknown to the millions of film-goers across the United States who lovingly called him 'The Prince of Whales', Fatty's good-natured buffoonery before the cameras masked a sinister – some would say diabolical – lust for booze and women. It was an explosive mix that one fateful night would cost him his career . . . and a young starlet her life.

What actually happened in that San Francisco hotel room remains a secret to this day. Only Fatty and pretty Virginia Rappe knew the real story. He never talked. She couldn't. But one thing is certain – it was the night Hollywood lost its innocence forever.

The weekend had begun innocently enough. It was early September, still summer in Los Angeles, and Fatty was looking forward to three days of rollicking fun far away from the harsh lights and demanding directors. On a morning like this, it felt good just to be alive. But as Fatty left his Tudor-style mansion that day he knew he had more to be thankful for than most. He had friends, money and fame. Only eight years earlier he had been a plumber's assistant, cleaning out drains for a few dollars a week.

But this was 1921, and Fatty was the king of comedy. He'd just signed a contract with Paramount Pictures to prove it. Three million dollars for three years – an incredible amount of money for those times.

The thirty-four-year-old star couldn't wait to celebrate his good fortune with friends and the ever-present throng of showgirls. He'd been planning this weekend for a long time. It was going to be special. Virginia, his adorable Virginia, would be there. Fatty had had his eye on her for some time, and with good reason. She was a stunning brunette from Chicago who didn't mind using her ample charms to get the break she craved. For Fatty, it was an irresistible combination.

Arbuckle had chosen San Francisco as the site for the revelry and on this

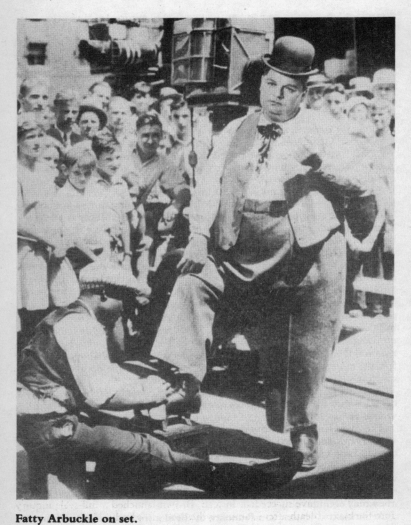

Fatty Arbuckle on set.

morning, Saturday, 3 September, he and his friends loaded themselves into two cars for the 450 mile journey to the bay city.

Arriving late that night, Fatty took three adjoining suites at the plush Hotel Saint Francis. As soon as the crates of bootleg liquor arrived, the comic star turned on the radio, fiddling with the dials before settling on the swinging sounds of a local jazz station. The party was under way.

For the next forty-eight hours it continued to pick up pace and, by Monday, there were as many as fifty revellers, in various states of undress. They toasted the good health of their boozy host, who stumbled about the room in his pyjamas and bathrobe swapping jokes and spilling drinks.

Eventually, Fatty made his way over to Virginia, who'd been throwing back her fair share of gin, and persuaded her to join him in the bedroom of suite 1221. As they left the room, the balloon-bellied comic winked to his friends and said: 'This is the chance I've waited for for a long time.'

Everyone laughed and wished him well.

Minutes later, above the merriment and music coming from the adjoining room, Virginia Rappe screamed for her life. An uneasy silence fell over the party, as guests strained to hear the ugly sounds coming from the bedroom. Suddenly, Virginia let out another blood-curdling scream. The revellers froze. Then the moans began. Loud, agonizing moans.

A laughing Arbuckle, by now a grotesque caricature of the jolly screen clown, walked back into the party room, his pyjamas ripped and torn.

'Go in and get her dressed ... She makes too much noise,' he laughingly told his stunned friends.

As Fatty swayed by the bedroom door, Virginia screamed again. This time, his smirk turned to a sneer. 'Shut up or I'll throw you out of the window,' he yelled.

Two of Virginia's friends, Bambina Delmont and Alice Blake, went into the bedroom. What they saw haunted them for the rest of their lives. The once-bubbly beauty lay almost naked on the bed, writhing in agony. Her clothes, which had been brutally torn from her body, were scattered about the floor. As they tried to comfort her, Virginia sobbed: 'I'm dying, I'm dying. He hurt me.'

Five days later, the twenty-five-year-old starlet was dead. Before she died, however, she managed to speak one more time, whispering to a startled nurse: 'Fatty Arbuckle did this to me. Please see that he doesn't get away with it.'

But Fatty and his powerful Hollywood friends did their best to hush the sordid story, and if it wasn't for an incorruptible coroner, Michael Brown, they may well have succeeded. Instead, Brown launched a full-scale inquiry into the bizarre death after examining the dead girl's body. He found that her female organs had been severely traumatized, causing death from peritonitis.

Following a police investigation, Arbuckle, who never showed any remorse over the girl's death, was formally charged with rape and murder. Hollywood, indeed the entire United States, went into shock. Was the king of comedy really a perverted Jekyll-and-Hyde monster?

The tabloids of the time believed so, and they had a field day publishing the lurid 'details' of the infamous weekend. During Arbuckle's first trial in November 1921, one of the most frequent rumours to find its way into print was that Virginia had been ravaged by a champagne bottle. Others claimed that she had been fatally injured when the 266-pound actor leapt on top of her in frenzied passion. But that's all they were . . . rumours. And the jury, which had been constantly reminded by defence attorneys that the dead girl was no angel, needed proof Arbuckle had indeed caused Virginia's death. After forty-three hours, they voted ten–two for acquittal. A mistrial was called. The second trial, which this time ended ten–two for conviction, was also declared a mistrial.

In April 1922, Fatty had to face his peers yet again. It was third time lucky for him. Not only did the jurors take just one minute to find him not guilty, but they also apologized to him, saying 'there was not the slightest proof to connect him in any way with a criminal wrong doing'!

As he left the courtroom, an obviously relieved Arbuckle, who went broke paying for his three defences, said in a solemn voice: 'My innocence of the hideous charges preferred against me has been proved . . . I am truly grateful to my fellow men and women. My life has been devoted to the production of clean pictures for the happiness of children. I shall try to enlarge my field of usefulness so that my art shall have a wider service.'

He never got the chance. In the eyes of twelve jurors, Fatty was innocent. In the eyes of the United States, however, he was guilty. Ironically, the three million dollar film contract which had indirectly led to his downfall, was torn up, and Arbuckle went into an enforced, drunken retirement.

What really did happen that late summer night? Two years before his death in 1933, Fatty was arrested for drunk driving by Hollywood police. As the officers approached the car, the fallen idol threw a bottle from the car, laughing in their faces: 'There goes the evidence!'

Was he somehow, through the murky haze of alcoholism, thinking back to that warm San Francisco night, of another bottle sent hurtling out of the twelfth storey window?

It was a secret Arbuckle took with him to the grave.

Thelma Todd – the Ice Cream Blonde

On the night of Sunday 15 December 1935, bubbly comedienne Thelma Todd attended a lavish party at the swish Hollywood nightclub, the Trocadero. It was one of the hottest tickets in town and fittingly, the beautiful comic star was the guest of honour – however this was to be the last party the so-called Ice Cream Blonde would ever attend. The next time her friends would see her, there would be no laughter, no Christmas cheer, no clinking of cocktail glasses ... only the quiet murmurs of sadness as they filed past her coffin.

What actually happened in the eight hours between the time the effervescent Thelma left the party and the time her limp body was discovered in her garage, one can only guess. There were many clues and contradictory stories, as well as whispers of drug trafficking, gambling and even the possible involvement of Charles 'Lucky' Luciano, the first Godfather of organized crime, and a man feared by studio bosses and politicians alike. And yet, the case of the Ice Cream Blonde remains shrouded in secrecy. It is a mystery Hollywood never solved – or forgot.

According to initial police investigations at the time, Thelma was chauffeured home following the swinging evening at the Trocadero. She had walked up the long stairway to the apartment she shared with her lover, director Roland West, while her driver watched to make sure she entered safely. The next time anyone saw her for certain – apart from her killer – was slumped behind the wheel of her chocolate-coloured Lincoln convertible, the blood dripping from her mouth on to her silver-and-blue evening gown and expensive mink coat. The ignition switch was on, but the motor was dead. So too was the delicious comedienne, whose flowing blonde locks and light-headed antics in film comedies with such superstars as the Marx Brothers and Laurel and Hardy had won her a legion of fans. She was just thirty years old.

Following a lengthy police inquiry, which uncovered a baffling array of contradictory evidence, the grand jury which investigated the death delivered a curious verdict – death by asphyxiation due to carbon monoxide poisoning. The conclusion, which left many questions unanswered, suggested that Thelma may have committed suicide. Yet why would Thelma want to kill

135

Thelma Todd lies in state.

herself? She had everything to live for – a successful career, scores of friends, money. In fact, actress Ida Lupino, a close friend who had been at the fateful Trocadero party, said Thelma seemed on top of the world that night, even gleefully telling her closest friends that she had taken a new lover, a San Francisco businessman, behind West's back. And if she had committed suicide, as implausible as that was, why was blood found on her mouth and clothes? And, strangest of all, why had several credible eye-witnesses claimed to have seen Thelma very much alive driving through Hollywood with an unidentified man beside her, after the party? Who was this dark stranger? Could it have been West, or maybe even the murderer? Were they the same person? Where were he and Thelma going at such a late hour? None of these questions was ever fully answered, despite the grand jury investigation and the lengthy police inquiry.

However, later it was revealed that West, who together with Thelma co-owned a smart neighbourhood restaurant favoured by movie stars, did eventually admit to the authorities – but only after a lengthy grilling – that he and the actress had a blazing row after she returned home from the party. But West told investigators he threw Thelma out of the apartment, and did not kill her. Other residents in the neighbourhood backed up West's story. They told police they heard a screaming Thelma pounding and kicking on front door of the apartment – leaving fresh kick marks which were later verified – before storming off into the night. West, it seemed, had an airtight alibi. But amateur sleuths always suspected that the director had staged the whole scene – just like one of his movies. According to them, West used a look-alike Thelma to play out the row in front of startled neighbours – while inside he quietly knocked out the real Thelma before stuffing her in the car and turning on the ignition. Supporters of this scenario claim West had long wanted to end the often-stormy affair, and keep the prized restaurant for himself. (Alas, like all the other theories, it was never proven, though in 1976, Pat Di Cicco, the once-powerful Hollywood agent and Thelma's former husband, said that he always believed West was behind the killing. (West was never to make another picture and died a forgotten man in 1952.) Meanwhile, not long after Thelma had been laid to rest amid much publicity, her lawyer was demanding a second inquest which he claimed would prove what he always suspected: that the happy-go-lucky comedienne had been bumped off by professional hit men working under orders from 'Lucky' Luciano. Luciano, the most powerful New York gangster of his day, had been expanding his empire into bars, clubs and restaurants up and down the Californian coast, setting up illegal gambling dens in back rooms. And it was no secret that emissaries from the evil Luciano had once approached Thelma seeking her permission to open a casino on the top floor of her restaurant. Luciano believed Thelma's rich, carefree friends would flock to the den. She refused, however, and Luciano was not known for giving people second chances. According to the lawyer, the moment Thelma turned 'Lucky' down, she became a marked woman, and it was only a matter of time before she was killed. As plausible as this theory was, the Luciano connection hardly saw the light of day, let alone the inside of a courtroom. Before any real inquiry had begun, the investigation was unceremoniously dropped. It seems the studio bosses, who wisely feared the all-powerful mobster and his ties to the film industry, eventually persuaded the lawyer to let the matter rest in peace.

And so the investigations into the mysterious death of Thelma Todd, the one-time grammar school teacher who found fame and fortune among the bright lights of Hollywood, were consigned to the massive scrap heap of criminal history.

It was a sad ending for the vivacious woman with the turquoise blue eyes who had thrilled movie-goers in films as warm hearted, vital and gay as she herself had been.

Mary Astor's Diary

Unlike so many of her contemporaries, actress Mary Astor not only survived the public airing of some of her most intimate secrets, she actually fared much better after her love life had been exposed. Such are the vagaries of a fickle public.

Mary, the fluttery-eyed murderess in the 1941 mystery classic, *The Maltese Falcon*, had one life-long friend – her diary, in which she faithfully confided every day. Now this may be a harmless hobby for a starry-eyed young girl growing up in the wheat fields of Illinois, but for a lust-filled screen siren it could, and would, prove to be dynamite. Newspapers of the day didn't call it 'the little blue book' because of its colourful binding, and its contents became 'must reading' in tabloids across the nation. The public just couldn't get enough and, as its revelations came tumbling out, newspaper circulation managers reached heights of ecstasy not unlike those Mary wrote about.

Eventually, the diary would become the most talked-about book of its time, causing a delicious uproar from Hollywood to New York. Guessing the likely 'stars' of Mary's prose became a national past-time, as did filling in the asterisks which covered Mary's sometimes 'colourful' language.

But the identities of all but two men remain secret to this day – and so does the whereabouts of the diary itself, which has become as elusive as the legendary Maltese Falcon. Yet if it hadn't been for a pair of misplaced cufflinks, the world may never have even known about the diary's existence ... let alone its incredible contents.

It was 1935, and Mary, a delicate beauty with a sophisticated grace, was involved in a torrid extramarital affair with playwright George S. Kaufman, whom she had met during a trip to New York. Following every one of their encounters, Mary would rush home to her diary and begin writing furiously about that day's love-making in rhapsodic detail.

Despite its explicit contents, however, Mary inexplicably took no pains to hide the book, and instead kept it in a drawer of her bedroom – the bedroom she sometimes shared with her husband, Dr Franklyn Thorpe. It was a careless mistake Mary would come to rue dearly.

One day, as the good doctor was looking around for his errant cuff links, he came across the diary and, being the inquisitive type, decided to take a peek at his wife's innermost secrets. The contents wounded what hurt most – his pride. It didn't take Dr Thorpe long to realize that he was not the Casanova

The seductive Mary Astor.

being written about. As he continued reading, he discovered the superman to be none other than Kaufman, a witty, though otherwise bland New Yorker. One can imagine how the poor physician felt as he sat on his bed, poring over Mary's exquisite memories.

In one very descriptive passage, Thorpe learned that his wife's affair with Kaufman had continued even after Mary got home to Hollywood from the visit to New York. Kaufman, not wanting to be far from the action, had conveniently set up his winter headquarters in nearby Palm Springs, and Thorpe soon found that all those trips Mary had made to the studio for 'costume fittings' were actually ruses to meet with her lover.

Dr Thorpe soon discovered that Mary's affair with Kaufman had been bubbling away merrily for over a year. But there were other names in the book as well, including a list of the best lovers in Hollywood – a list Mary had compiled from personal experience – including screen legend John Barrymore. Just who else was included on the list was never revealed, but it sent shock waves throughout the movie industry and allegedly sent some very prominent actors running for cover.

Of course, to Dr Thorpe, one name was more than enough to send him into a frenzied jealousy. He demanded Mary end the affair, but the defiant actress, unable to do without Kaufman's considerable charms, promptly told him what he could do with that suggestion. Not surprisingly, the doctor, who had wisely held on to the diary, demanded and was granted a divorce. He then went after custody of their four-year-old daughter, Marylyn. While Mary may not have contested the divorce proceedings too strongly, she was prepared to fight all out to retain custody of the child.

In the down-and-dirty struggle which ensued, Dr Thorpe began leaking selected passages of the saucy diary to the press, while Mary sat on the witness stand in tears. The public was agog, but Astor's lovers were aghast lest they be named. Kaufman's friends reported that he tore his hair out and cried that he was being crucified as the revelations about him and Mary came tumbling out, while John Barrymore vanished into an asylum. In addition, a deputation of Hollywood tycoons, some of them rumoured to be in the book, visited Astor and begged her to withdraw her claim to Marylyn.

Astor refused, risking her reputation and career, and so the scandal continued, as Thorpe leaked more and more pages, until Judge 'Goody' Knight, who was presiding over the custody battle, ordered the diary impounded as 'pornography'. The public, to say nothing of the newspaper editors, was dismayed.

But with his most explosive ammunition now in the hands of the court, Thorpe, whose own philandering was no secret in Hollywood, was fighting a losing battle. Indeed, his maid testified that on four successive nights, he had four different showgirls share his bed. The court, which by now had had about all it could take of bedroom antics, decided that Thorpe was no saint himself, and ordered that the child spend nine months of the year with Mary, and the three-month summer vacation with her father. However, much to Mary's dismay, the judge steadfastly refused to return her beloved diary.

What actually became of the diary is still a mystery. In 1952, it was reportedly burned, but stories persist to this day that it still exists, as phantom like as the Maltese Falcon.

According to the late New York journalist Howard Teichmann, the diary was never destroyed as reported by the wire services, but was locked in an underground vault of the *Daily News* newspaper which mysteriously acquired it many years ago. After Mary's death in 1987, a team of reporters from the newspaper scoured the files looking for the lost legend, but found only some correspondence between editors of the paper and Astor's ex-husband. Unfortunately, the editors who might have had first-hand knowledge of the diary's whereabouts and therefore be able to shed some light on one of Hollywood's most enduring mysteries are now dead.

The diary's final resting place, and the identities of Mary's many lovers, remain among Hollywood's most vexing mysteries.

Chapter Six

SECRETS OF THE PAST

What is the secret of Stonehenge, the great circle of gaunt stones which stand as lonely sentinels on Salisbury Plain? Who constructed the baffling Money Pit which man has been trying to excavate for 200 years? and what happened to an entire population who mysteriously vanished from an ancient Mexican city?

The Money Pit

Buried treasure is the stuff of boyhood dreams — doubloons, sovereigns, gold ingots — buried in the sand by pirates or plunderers, waiting to be discovered centuries afterwards by intrepid explorers. Sadly for most it remains a dream. But on a tiny island in Mahone Bay, off the coast of Nova Scotia, is a huge hole in the ground where just such treasure may have been buried. Trying to discover the secrets it holds has cost the lives and fortunes of men obsessed with the thought that within its confines lies untold riches. The Money Pit of Oak Island is one of the most enduring mysteries of all time . . .

It is in 1795 that the story of the Money Pit begins, when Daniel McGinnis, a sixteen-year-old farmer's son, gently paddled his canoe across the placid water to the hour-glass shaped Oak Island — so named because of the dense growth of mature oak trees which flourished across it. The island, crossed by a stretch of stagnant swampland, is just one of many in Mahone Bay which McGinnis, intent on a picnic and a spot of solitary fishing, alighted on by chance. The boy went ashore, gathered his picnic basket and rod and moved inland to deposit them under the shade of one of the oaks. He found, in a small clearing, a gnarled old tree with the tell-tale grooves in its bark indicating where a block-and-tackle system for hauling or lowering had been in place. Below the tree was a circular impression in the earth, an indentation which seemed to the boy as if a hole had been dug and then filled in rapidly. The replaced earth had not been stamped down hard enough to conceal all signs of digging. Daniel was convinced that he had hit on a clearing where buried treasure had been hidden away!

The lad forgot his fishing expedition and paddled back to the mainland to breathlessly tell his pals about what he had seen. Gathering picks and shovels, he and friends Anthony Vaughan, thirteen, and John Smith, twenty prepared for a return visit the following day.

Digging into the earth was testimony that McGinnis had been right. They found themselves burrowing down into some kind of chamber, the sides bearing pick and shovel marks of long ago. When they had gone down just over a metre they struck a smooth-faced flagstone. Scraping away across the floor of the pit they realized that they had discovered an entire floor of such stones. Underneath, they dreamed, must be the treasure. But when the heavy stones were prised from the clay, there was nothing but more earth. Over the

The Money Pit in recent years.

course of the following week they continued digging and at three metres, six metres and nine metres hit a flooring of closely packed logs, the gaps between filled with coconut fibres. By nine metres the disillusioned but intrigued youngsters decided to abandon their venture. In the way of all excited young men, they pledged an oath to return – and unlike most of these hastily made, hastily broken pledges, one of them kept their word, returning to the island nine years later for a more thorough, scientific excavation of the pit. Nothing had dented John Smith's certain knowledge that deep in the shaft lay treasure.

Smith secured the financial backing of a syndicate, comprised of local businessmen, but funded chiefly by Simeon Lynds, a well-to-do local landowner. When they got back to Oak Island the shaft looked much as they had left it all those years before. Using the money from the syndicate, a workforce was raised among local farm labourers and work began in earnest, digging deeper and deeper towards the glittering prize which Smith knew was there. More oak platforms with their coconut fibre matting were struck at twelve metres, fifteen metres and eighteen metres – the latter having putty as well as the fibre between the cracks in the logs. At just over twenty one metres they hit a covering of plain oak, at just over twenty four metres another platform of putty-sealed oak and at just over twenty seven metres a stone – not of indigenous Nova Scotia rock – which bore an inscription that could not be made out. Smith, a successful businessman in his own right by then, had actually purchased the whole island. He took the stone and put it in pride of place over his hearth, the significance, if any, of the almost illegible script completely lost on him.

After the stone was wrenched free, another layer of wood lay underneath. Finally, although there was no reason to suggest why, the syndicate thought that under this wood lay the caskets of treasure. They resolved to rest for the night for a final surge in the morning which would make them wealthy. They were all of the mind that twenty four hours would not make any difference to riches which had lain there for so long.

In fact the men left the pit for forty eight hours – the following day was Sunday, and Smith declared no work on the Sabbath. On Monday morning the men returned to the pit – to find it flooded to within ten metres of the top. They frantically began bailing using an outmoded pump bought by the syndicate from an old oilfield. Their efforts were in vain; no matter how hard they pumped or how furiously they bailed, the water stayed a constant ten metres below the lip of the shaft entrance. It was defeat bitter enough to make them abandon the shaft for a year.

The following spring they hit upon a new idea; burrowing a separate shaft alongside the original to a depth of thirty-three-and-a-half metres. Then they planned to break through and release the water into the surplus pit and then resume work on the treasure hunt. All went well until the final stages when the walls of the new hole suddenly caved in, hurling tons of water and earth on to the diggers. They were lucky to escape without loss of life and injury. That pit too flooded to a depth of ten metres from the top. Smith and his partners finally conceded defeat to the forces of nature, reasoning that an underground spring of such force lay beneath the site that they were never likely to reach their goal.

The next assault on the Money Pit came in 1849 when a new consortium of wealthy businessmen was formed. Called The Truro Syndicate – taking their name from the Cornwall district once rich in tin mines – they included in their ranks Anthony Vaughan, who had once again become intrigued by the treasure island he first dug on all those years ago. Dr David Lynds, a relative of Simeon Lynds, was also one of the backers.

The first shaft was drained using more modern, powerful pumps and cleared out completely. There seemed to be no problem with water or clearing out the debris from the caved-in second shaft to a depth of just over twenty six metres. But again, after calling a halt on Saturday night and returning on Monday morning the syndicate found that the shaft was completely flooded – again just ten metres from the top. After several more pumping and bailing methods, the syndicate decided to use a drill that was driven by a horse which -would bore through the different layers below. Borings from the drill produced clay, gravel, mud and sand. To the east of the pit, at a depth of thirty two metres, they discovered fragments of oak, fifty six centimetres of metal, more oak and finally a bed of spruce before finally hitting the clay bed again. A faint jarring motion on the drill as it went down made the searchers believe they had brushed past two treasure chests.

Next occurred one of those puzzling episodes for which a completely satisfactory answer has never been found. The drilling foreman, James Pitblado, was accused by one of the tough labourers of taking something shiny from the drill bit as he ran his calloused hands through it after it was brought to the surface. The labourer who witnessed this incited the other men to believe Pitblado had pocketed a jewel of some kind and they demanded that he produce the gem at a meeting. Pitblado refused, saying he would announce his discovery, whatever it may have been, to the directors of the syndicate the next time a meeting was held. Pitblado then tried to buy the entire eastern-end of Oak Island, away from the Money Pit. He was unsuccessful in his venture and vanished shortly afterwards – the riddle of what he pocketed still unanswered.

In 1850 a new shaft was dug. That too flooded – but this time a curious labourer tasted the water on his hands. He was curious about the popular underground-stream theory because the heavy clay, like that on his farm, was impervious to water. Tasting the water gave the searchers the clue they were seeking about the flooding pit – it was seawater. On a nearby beach the syndicate unearthed another of the amazing secrets of the Money Pit.

'As the tide receded the sand seemed to suck the water down, like it was thirsty,' noted one syndicate member James Bolton. They excavated the sand to discover a truly remarkable engineering feat. Whoever had originally dug the money pit had ensured its safety by an intricate system designed to flood it if intruders came close to penetrating its secrets. A tunnel of stones, sealed over with kelp grass and coconut fibre, led in a slanting direction from the beach to the money pit. The grass and fibre kept out sand which would have clogged the tunnel but allowed the water to run freely through it. The stone tunnel led straight back to the pit, entering the shaft at a depth of thirty metres. As long as the pit stayed full of earth, the water would be kept out. But as soon as the diggers reached it, the water burst through as high-tide was reached, keeping the secrets of the pit safe. Smith had not been beaten by

145

nature but by a carefully designed and built man-made security system.

At first the prospectors tried damming the tunnel, a solution that failed when it was smashed by an unusually high tide. Then they tried to block the tunnel completely by digging yet another shaft near to the site of the original. Water flooded in at a depth of just under eleven metres after the labourers had dislodged a boulder. The party thought they had intercepted the tunnel from the beach, but they were not deep enough and should have realized it. Wood was driven into the soft earth to stem the flow of the water and yet another shaft was dug. At thirty six metres they tunnelled sideways into the original shaft – and the whole thing collapsed, again miraculously without loss of life. Another nine years passed before the syndicate returned – again with no success. More shafts were sunk and flooded. And the Money Pit claimed its first victim – a worker scalded to death when a steam pump blew up.

After the Truro Syndicate abandoned its operations, hopeful treasure hunters spurred on by the lure of great wealth arrived like locusts on the island. Soon the area around the pit resembled a pock-marked moon surface with countless shafts and holes. One man even attempted to swim to the bottom of the flooded original shaft using primitive diving apparatus!

The next assault on the secret was made in 1866 by the Halifax Syndicate which ascertained that the water entered the shaft at a depth of thirty three metres and that the mouth of the tunnel was just over one metre high, and just under one metre wide. One of the Halifax team, said: 'I saw enough to convince me that there was treasure buried there and enough to convince me that they will never get it.' Blair was right. The Halifax Syndicate folded after investing £20,000 in an effort to pump out the water which stood as sentinel to whatever lay at the base of the pit.

In 1891 the search passed on to the Oak Island Treasure Company which was headed by Frederick Leander Blair. He organized one assault on the original shaft but when that failed, the pit lay dormant for seven years as the syndicate struggled to raise more money. It wasn't until 1897 that the excavation began again at the mouth of the flood tunnel. Nearly seventy kilogrammes of dynamite was lowered into the mouth of the tunnel and detonated to prevent further flooding. They drained the pit, came back the next day – and found it flooded again! Then, using a drill encased in piping to ensure smoother operating, a bore was lowered into the murky depths. At thirty eight metres it bit into a sheet of iron. A smaller drill was passed down and this drilled through the obstruction to a depth of forty six metres, passing en-route through some soft stone. Fifty three centimetres below that it hit some oak, then hit more metal, and a fragment of parchment. When the parchment was examined on the surface it contained the letters V.I. When the engineers attempted to insert piping down the length of the drill to obtain further samples, the bit was deflected, and water rushed up the bore pipe at enormous pressure. Blair, thinking that he had struck yet another water-barrier that the ingenious mind behind the construction of the Pit had devised, poured in red dye and ordered labourers to watch the sea. Sure enough, red dye seeped into the sea in three different areas, confirming more water barriers constructed to keep the pit from the reach of man. The syndicate sunk fourteen more shafts in a bid to block the tunnels, failing in their plan and turning the area around the pit into a maze of holes and swamps. The syndicate bankrupted itself soon after.

The next plan came in 1909 when rich engineer Captain Henry Bowdoin invested £30,000 in a new drill. He failed. Then in 1912 a madcap boffin tried a scheme to freeze all the water in the pit and hack it out with picks. He too failed. For the next twenty years the D-I-Y prospectors picked over the ravaged site, the original shaft barely discernable from the countless other pits and holes which dotted the area. In the 1930s several schemes were formulated by wealthy businessmen. One involved rigging up a system of steel pylons ringing the site to keep out the water, another sending divers in a diving bell to the water's depths. Only one explorer distinguished himself from the others with their madcap schemes – an adventurer called Gilbert Hedden who found a large triangular pile of stones on a deserted beach near to where the original tunnel was located. There was also an arrow pointed towards where the Money Pit lay. Hedden, using a chart he claimed was printed in a book called *Captain Kidd and his Skeleton Island*, which chronicled the exploits of one of history's most infamous pirates, said his discovery proved conclusively that the treasure was the property of the infamous pirate. While many subscribed to Hedden's theory, others poured scorn on it.

Hedden was followed by engineer Edwin Hamilton who drilled the deepest shaft of fifty five metres, and discovered that the second tunnel entered the pit at forty six metres on the opposite of the original flood tunnel. In 1963 the next casualties of the mystifying hole occurred when on 17 August Robert Restall was overcome by the exhaust fumes of his water pump, killing him, his father and two other men who tried to rescue them. In 1965 a geologist, Robert Dunfield, squandered £120,000 in digging more new holes, without any success.

To this day the secrets of the Money Pit have not been penetrated. One author, Rupert Furneaux, in his authoritative account of the island entitled *Money Pit: the Mystery of Oak Island*, speculates that the British Army buried the treasure there during the American War of Independence. But there are no records of such an undertaking. The secret lies intact in the mud and clay of that lonely little island.

The Secret City

No traveller to Mexico City can fail to be awed by both its achievements and its ghastly pollution. Sitting in an enormous bowl in the earth, the smoke and fumes belched out by its millions of citizens and their cars, factories and fires makes for an acrid haze which hangs over the city like an impenetrable screen. Only when it rains does the haze disappear momentarily. In such an environment it is no wonder that most visitors 'escape' from Mexico City to another metropolis – the secret city of Teotihuacan.

In this magnificent place there is no pollution – for the simple reason that it is a dead city, abandoned mysteriously by its people centuries ago. The race which built Teotihuacan on the plains outside modern-day Mexico City displayed a skill equal to that of the pyramid builders of ancient Egypt, and brought a level of culture to the Americas that was undreamed of in Europe at that time. But the great edifices of the pyramids of the Sun and the Moon which stand at the top of its broad cobbled avenues, its intricate carvings and ornately decorated palaces, leave no clue to the people who built and inhabited it – a people who left without a trace, twenty centuries ago. Just what the secrets of Teotihuacan are is a puzzle which has fascinated and confounded historians ever since the city was first discovered.

The builders of the city of Teotihuacan – the name given to the place by people who inhabited it long after its founders had disappeared – were highly religious and raised the massive structures in reverence to ancient gods. They treated their dead with a respect that Christians would admit was civilized and created magnificent artefacts which have been unearthed over the years. At its peak, some quarter of a million people lived in Teotihuacan over a vast plateau which stands some 2,250 metres above sea level. Indeed, even though the broad-sweeping avenues and tall pyramids give an impression of a great city, archaeologists estimate that nine-tenths of Teotihuacan lies buried under the dirt and shifting sands blown over its structures through the centuries. At its height it stretched over twenty three square kilometres!

It was the Aztecs, that other great Mexican civilization, who, stumbling on the ruins of Teotihuacan a thousand years after its decline, named it. In their language Teotihuacan means 'The place of those who have the road of the Gods'. The Aztecs, although they adapted the ruins of the city for their own purposes and way of life, were just as baffled as to who the mysterious race

The secret city of Teotihuacan.

was which originally had constructed the city of Teotihuacan.

Teotihuacan's main thoroughfare is called The Avenue of the Dead which leads up to the mighty Pyramid of the Sun. There is another pyramid at the northern end of the Avenue called Pyramid of the Moon; both structures signifying the great importance the founders placed on paying homage to the two great forces ruling their lives. Of the two, the Pyramid of the Sun is the tallest, aligned on an east-west axis that reflects the path of the sun across the sky. It is generally believed that the pyramid was constructed to symbolize the universe, with its four corners representing the points of the compass and its apex representing the 'heart of life'. Its sides measure 225 metres at the base and it is seventy metres high. Experts estimate that there are some two and a half million tonnes of dried brick and rubble constituting its body – and that it would have taken 3,000 men thirty years to complete!

The Pyramid of the Moon is smaller, some forty three metres high, and faces an open space which was called The Plaza of the Moon. Here, ancient rites in praise of the dark forces were performed, although there has been little evidence unearthed over the years to suggest that the people practised human sacrifice. Archaeological exploration has revealed several layers of the city, built during the eight hundred or so years it flourished.

For historians, the most striking constructions are the palaces, particularly the Temple of the Feathered Serpent God. The temple, situated off of the Plaza of the Moon, would have been reached by the way of the Avenue of the Dead, the thoroughfare on which stood the houses of the city's elite; the priests, craftsmen, minor functionaries and the leaders themselves. The remainder of the population lived in the surrounding areas – testified to by the huge numbers of wattle and daub hut remains found under the earth.

At the height of its power, the walls of the city shone with beautiful frescoes which testified to the artistic development, even genius, of the population. Other items found there include a tripod vase, graceful eating bowls and implements, and numerous figures depicting fertility, the seasons and death. The inhabitants developed a system of writing – which, unlike hieroglyphics – still has to be fully understood, and also a system of numeracy. Aztec, Toltec and Mayan cultures in Mexico did not use systems similar to those discovered in the ruins of Teotihuacan.

Researchers think that the wattle-and-daub hut remains could have been there much longer than the city itself – suggesting that there was a settlement of primitive people there in prehistoric times whose labour was harnessed by a cultured, more intelligent race to build the magnificent edifices which remain to this day. Frenchman Desiré Charnay, credited with being the first European to stumble across the site in 1880, believed it to be a Toltec ruin. But exploreres after him have ruled out the Toltecs – they merely adopted 'squatters' rights' over the buildings when they arrived around the first century A.D.

Mexican scholar Jimenez Moreno argued that the city was built by a priestly autocracy, the like of which has not been witnessed in other parts of Mexico. He argues that the numbers of buildings erected to religious figures, coupled with the pyramids of the Sun and the Moon, point towards an educated priest-class who ruled over workers who toiled in the surrounding fields on the fertile plain. Remains of maize, wheat, barley, beans and other vegetable produce found on the different layers of the city testify that it was once a huge market area as well as a great metropolis. Jimenez says the Temple of the Feathered Serpent God signifies the union of heaven, earth, land and water and suggests that the whole city may be one gigantic monument to the gods – thanking them for blessing the surrounding region with abundant crops, water and wildlife. Another Frenchman, Laurette Sejourne, concurs, stating that religious symbols and artefacts found in most of the buildings indicate that it was a giant 'cloistered' city, with the workers and artesans living in the hut villages on the outskirts.

Nobles in the city lived in separate complexes, off the Avenue of the Dead. One of these complexes, called Zacuala, covered an area of some 3300 square metres and had its own private temples. The casual visitor to these gracious buildings is reminded that they were flourishing at a time when the Huns, Goths and Vandals were turning Europe into rivers of blood! Like the Romans, the original inhabitants of the city invented a drainage system which provided fresh water, but which could be plugged if supplies ran low. Beneath the houses were found human remains, burned, wrapped in linen shrouds, presumably placed in these home-made crypts after being blessed by the priests. The inhabitants placed great significance on the death ceremony, garnishing the burial area with statuettes and tools for the deceased's life.

One professor who has devoted much of his academic life to the study of Teotihuacan is Rene Millon of the University of New York at Rochester. He thinks that the hut dwellers eventually left the outskirts of the city to seek the sanctuary of the stone dwellings within. He bases his findings on evidence of a withdrawal from the plain around about A.D. 150. But what he and others have been unable to ascertain is the reason for the mass exodus of the city's population. There have been no signs of a great fire, no evidence of a plague, no sackings or mass killings. One author in the 1950s put forward the theory that the priests were overthrown by the peasantry in a year of famine.

The truth is, the secrets of Teotihuacan are as safe now as they were when the mysterious race who built this most incredible city vanished forever.

Secrets of the Standing Stones

They stand as mighty symbols of a time that modern man barely comprehends. The scant knowledge gleaned of ages when the massive stones were formed, has been unearthed through archaeological studies and examination of artefacts left behind. No records exist to tell us what made the ancient inhabitants of Salisbury Plain build the circling stones which are the enduring legacy of not-so-primitive man. And no pot, pan or flint head, valuable though they are, can express the brooding, dark secrets of that age when the most famous of all the megaliths that span western Europe was constructed. Centuries on, the giants of Stonehenge still keep their secrets.

The ancient monument itself is but one of a number of megaliths – the word is Greek meaning great stones – which cut across Europe in a giant swathe. There are sites in Brittany, Malta and Spain, and 900 in the British Isles alone, the northernmost ones situated on the windswept Shetland Isles. But Stonehenge has come to symbolize the age of the megaliths, with all its sinister and mysterious connotations of human sacrifice, sun worship and pagan ritual. The monument itself was built in three distinct phases spanning a period of over 1,300 years. Each group that embarked on the mammoth task of hauling, carving and placing the stones, did not quite manage to complete their work – leaving the job to be finished by their successors.

Historians agree that the first builders were neolithic, beginning the original construction around 2700 B.C. These first hunter-warriors excavated the encircling ditch and erected the so-called heel stone, which is aligned so that the first rays of light from the sun on Midsummer's Day strike it and the central point of the inner stone circle. The same men dug the Aubrey Holes – the fifty six shallow pits which form a ring near the banked earth surrounding the structure at Stonehenge. When the pits were excavated earlier this century they contained a wealth of burned objects and charred bones – giving rise to one theory that the stones constituted a holy cremation ground for early man.

Eight hundred and fifty years after man began the first steps towards creating Stonehenge, the race called the Beaker People moved in to finish the massive stone legacy. The Beaker People – the name derived from their habit of burying their dead with ornate pots and vases – accomplished amazing engineering feats which have baffled and bemused modern technicians. Theirs is truly one of the great secrets of Stonehenge – for the Beaker People, equipped with flint head axes and without the use of the wheel – quarried rock from Wales and dragged it to Stonehenge! Over 480 kilometres from the hills of South Wales, to the plateau of Stonehenge, were dragged the enormous stones; eighty in all, each weighing more than four tonnes, the stones were assembled into a double circle. Just how the Beaker People accomplished such a feat with such primitive tools has baffled researchers.

No less impressive a feat occurred around 1500 B.C. when the Beaker People – who failed in their bid to finish the construction – were themselves succeeded by another, unamed generation, who harnessed the labour of an estimated 1,000 workers or slaves to drag quarried stones from the downs near modern-day Marlborough to the Stonehenge site. Historians can only concur that primitive sledges were used to haul the stones in an operation that would have taken months to complete. Once at the site, they were fashioned into the giant stones that exist as the Stonehenge we know. And these same craftsmen, who had devised no system that we know of to read, write or perform mathematics, created a system to lever into place the giant lintels which crown the upright stones. The means by which they did this is unknown, but Stonehenge man shared something in common with his fellow megalith builders in Europe and other parts of the British Isles; all the monuments are constructed using the same unit of measurement which has since become known as the Megalith Yard, a distance of 0.83 metres. How or why this common unit of measurement came to be used by these 'primitive' people is something that has not been satisfactorily explained.

The cult of Druidism is espoused by the heirs to the ancient Celtic priests, who lay claim to Stonehenge and each Summer Solstice are allowed access to the jealously guarded national monument to practise their ancient rites. But experts concur that it is too old to have been built by their forefathers, the original Druids.

The most widely accepted theory about the origins and construction of Stonehenge is that propounded by Oxford University professor Alexander Thom who, after a long days sailing on Loch Roag on the Isle of Lewis, off Scotland's bleak western coastline, stopped to gaze at the standing stones of Callanish, often dubbed Scotland's Stonehenge. He went ashore and, standing in the centre of the stones, checked the position of the Pole Star. By this he was able to determine that the structure was aligned due north–south. But because this monument was prehistoric, and was built in a time when the Pole Star's constellation had not reached its present position in the galaxy, Professor Thom reasoned that its architects must have had some other means of determining the alignment of the stones. Excited by his discovery, Professor Thom embarked on a journey throughout Britain and Europe to examine more than 600 standing stone sites. And they all proved his theory was correct – that the stones were, in fact, crude space observatories. All were built on the north-south axis, marking the moments throughout the calendar when the sun and moon rose and set.

In 1963, another professor, Gerald Hawkins, the professor of Astronomy at Boston University in the United States, took the Thom theory one step further and announced that Stonehenge was, in fact, a massive prehistoric computer, capable of complex calculations based on the heavens. 'The men that built it proved they were not primitive by dint of their architecture' he said. The published works of C.A. Newham followed on by stating that a caste of highly evolved astronomer-priests would have stood in the centre of the stones and tracked the path of the sun and moon by using the stones as a guide. Dr Euan Mackie of Glasgow's Hunterian Museum took the 'elite' caste system theory further along when he announced that he had found the stone-age 'university' where these priests may have lived and trained. Artefacts of woven cloth, remains of a rich diet and other objects found at Durrington Walls near Stonehenge were proof of the higher quality of life among a select few that distinguished them from their fellow men.

If what the academics say is true, then the widely held belief that Stonehenge was a place of pagan worship is inaccurate. It also means that, in a time when there was no numeracy or literacy, an intellectual elite existed within the stone age communities and, somehow, gleaned the knowledge to measure the megalithic yard and to chart planetary movements. Professor Sir Fred Hoyle, one of Britain's foremost astronomers, also supported the theory that Stonehenge was a giant observatory. He agreed with Hawkins' speculation that the stones could be used as markers to gauge the moon's activity as it passed through its lunar cycle. The Aubrey Holes, dug by the first workers on the site, were significant, said Hoyle; their number, fifty six, representing almost exactly three times the 18.6 years of the moon's cycle. When he fed this into a computer he found out that the stones could predict eclipses of the Sun! 'The construction demanded a level of intellectual attainment greater than the standard to be expected from a "primitive" community,' he said.

As to other theories about the mysterious stones, the enthusiast for mystery can choose any one of a number; that the site was a marker for aliens from outer space to land their craft; that it was a place where infertile women went to be blessed; that it was a temple for human sacrifice, an altar to the gods who saw over the harvest, or a forum for a primitive parliament.

Only those massive, immoveable stones know the true history of Stonehenge – and they can never reveal their secrets.

154

Secret Societies

The Ku Klux Klan

Of all the world's secret societies that have their origins in the past, few are more hated than the dreaded Ku Klux Klan.

Founded on Christmas Eve 1865, by former confederate General Nathan Forrest and five other Civil War veterans in Pularski, Tennessee, the Klan was originally formed to relieve the boredom of the post-war era by intimidating 'niggers'.

The General and his friends gave themselves preposterous titles, such as Grand Dragon and Imperial Wizard, and dressed themselves in white, hooded robes to shield their identities.

Within two years, the group, which by now comprised of hundreds of former slave owners and soldiers, was waging an all-out terror campaign against blacks across the southern states of America – intimidation of Jews and Catholics was soon to follow.

Using violence and threats, the KKK played a key role in shaping the beliefs and customs of the post-war deep South, using its considerable clout to influence elections and derail any legislation it considered detrimental to its aim of total white supremacy. The KKK also killed on a huge scale without fear of ever being caught, largely because no one knew the identities of the members, and those who did were sworn to secrecy. The penalty for breaking the Klan code of silence was death.

According to historians, more than 3500 blacks – men, women and children – were murdered in the Klan's first ten years of existence, as the shadowy organization spread its tentacles further and further across the defeated and demoralized southern states.

By the 1920s, at the height of its popularity, the Klan had about five million members, including doctors, lawyers, police officers, judges and other pillars of white society. Even the so-called 'liberal' northern states fell victim to the scourge, as Klan groups appeared in the industrial cities where there was a dwindling number of jobs and increasing local resentment at the number of immigrant workers. The Klan's burning crosses and hateful rhetoric struck fear in minority groups across the nation, and more than 900 blacks alone were lynched in the decade.

During the 1960s the Klan was also at the forefront of attacks on civil rights

A Klan member gives a menacing salute.

groups during a time when southern states were ordered by the federal government to desegregate their schools, hotels, bars and restaurants. Claiming they were going to protect 'the old way of life,' the KKK embarked on an all-out campaign to block the inevitable changes in civil rights. They lynched local blacks, bombed churches and burned down minority-owned farms and businesses. In 1964, Klansmen brazenly killed three civil rights workers as they drove across Mississippi trying to rally support for their cause.

As civil rights in the U.S. have improved over the years, membership of the Klan has dwindled – latest Government estimates put the number of Klansmen at about 7000 – however the KKK still has not forsaken its violent tactics. Its members still attack black families, peace activists and Jewish communities, and as recently as 1981 the Klan lynched a teenage black man.

Of most concern today, to law enforcement groups and civil liberty organizations, is the growing alliance between the KKK and the neo-Nazi movement. According to FBI reports, neo-Nazi attacks on minority groups have more than tripled in the past two years, and the group has been blamed for several racially-motivated murders.

The thugs, who have become virtual storm troopers for the older Klansmen, were brought into the racist fold by Tom Metzger, a long-time KKK operative and avowed white supremist. The neo-Nazis act as bodyguards at Klan rallies, and recently gained national notoriety when they started a studio brawl on a television show which was probing the re-emergence of hate groups in the United States.

The neo-Nazis have also learned the value of secrecy. Two years ago, when one of their comrades decided to leave and speak out against the group, he was nailed to a plank as a warning to any other would-be traitors.

As long as people hate simply because of a person's skin colour or religious beliefs, the white-robed Klansmen and the evil neo-Nazis will always be a blot on U.S. society.

The Mafia

From its humble beginnings many, many years ago in the small towns and villages of Sicily, the modern-day Mafia is probably the most feared – and dangerous – secret organization in the world. During its incredibly violent history, it has carved out a multi-billion dollar criminal empire dwarfing even the assets of the largest legitimate corporations, protecting its ill-gotten gains with murder, bribery, extortion and a code of silence: the *omerta*, which if broken is punishable by death.

Few men have ever lived to break the *omerta*, but in 1985, Tommaso Buscetta, a Mafia chief, revealed to a hushed New York courtroom the most secret rituals of the underworld crime Tzars.

'I was given a "saint" (a wallet-size picture of a saint with a small prayer printed underneath) and then my finger was pricked and I had to rub blood from my finger onto the saint and then set fire to it and I had to say the oath. After ... I was to say that if I should betray the organization, my flesh would burn like this saint.'

Buscetta also revealed that the mobsters regard themselves as 'men of honour,' who are sworn under penalty of death not to touch another Mafioso's wife or lie to another member.

According to law enforcement officials, the Mafia or Cosa Nostra – Italian for 'This Thing of Ours' – is made up of just a few thousand members, but has tens of thousands of associates. The Mafia gained a foothold in the United States when Italian immigrants arrived *en masse* during the early 1900s. In run-down areas of cities like New York and Chicago, young packs of hoodlums would extort money from their hard-working countrymen.

The rise of the Mafia, in the form we know it today, began with the murder of one of the first major syndicate bosses Nicholas Morello, leader of the Sicilian gangsters in New York, who was shot to death in September 1917. Following his execution, the two warring Mafia factions, those of Sicilian and Neapolitan descent, merged for the first time and operated under the leadership of Guiseppe 'Joe the Boss' Masseria for nearly a decade. Eventually, Masseria was executed by one of his top henchmen who, just five months later, was himself killed. The next day, forty old Mafia mobsters were murdered by killers loyal to a 'rising star' on the Mafia scene Charles 'Lucky' Luciano – the man credited with establishing the Mafia 'family' system in the United States.

Luciano carved New York City up into five criminal families, all headed by men he could trust – other cities across the nation soon followed suit. Within a decade, Luciano was known as the *Capo di tutti Capi* – Boss of All Bosses and the first Mafia Godfather. He also created 'the commission' – a mob board of directors made up from the heads of the families which decided who could become members of the clan, which family got what share of business and, when another mobster had to be executed.

The Prohibition years of the early 1930s fuelled the mob's financial coffers and political clout, as the nation turned to the bootleggers for its booze. Thugs like Al Capone and Frank Nitty rose to incredible heights of power during those violent days, when the Mafia families virtually controlled the cities in which they were based. It was said that Capone ruled every senior politician, judge and police officer in Chicago during Prohibition.

After Congress repealed Prohibition in 1933, the Mafia began to look at new ways to make money, and quickly became more involved in drugs and gambling. Las Vegas, it has been said, was built by mob money.

During the 1940s, 1950s and 1960s, scores of mobsters were ordered to be 'taken out' by rival gangsters as the battles for new sources of revenue heated up across the country. Leadership succession was shaped to a large degree by assassinations. One of the most ruthless hit men of the period was Albert Anastasia, who headed the infamous 'Murder Incorporated' which hired itself out to whoever could afford the 'special' services it offered. Anastasia, like many of his peers, was himself eventually murdered. He was shot to death in October, 1957, while he sat in the barber shop of a New York hotel.

Although the family system of Mafia rule has survived to the present day, federal prosecutors and law enforcement officials have scored recent successes against the organization, and have put four of the five heads of the New York city families in jail. However, authorities predict a new breed of leaders will soon emerge and fear a new wave of battles, as mobsters fight for power.

The only New York City family boss still active in the day-to-day operations of his syndicate is John Gotti – head of the Gambino family – and the modern-day 'boss of all bosses'. He controls an estimated 250 hard-core members and hundreds more associates. Police believe Gotti was behind the execution of Paul Castellano, his immediate predecessor. Castellano was gunned down in December, 1985, as he pulled up outside a Manhattan restaurant. To no one's surprise, the three killers have never been identified.

The Masons

Not all the world's secret societies are committed to crime, violence or other forms of chaos. In fact one of the oldest and largest of the secret groups, the Freemasons, was originally formed to protect the professional and religious interests of a particular group of craftsmen – the stonemasons.

In spite of what some masons may proclaim however, the beginnings of Freemasonry do not go back to the Biblical days of King Solomon. On the contrary, the organization was founded in London, in 1717, at the Goose and Gridiron Tavern. Throughout the previous century, membership in guilds of men actually working as stonemasons, began to decline rapidly. To bolster their dwindling membership, the masons opened their doors to honorary members, who became known as Freemasons.

The exact origins of the name 'freemason' is shrouded in mystery, although it has been in use for several centuries. Some scholars believe the word stems from the fact that masons were free from feudal serfdom, while others believe it points to a worker who fashioned freestone. Regardless, within sixteen years, borrowing rituals and symbols from many ancient sources, the number of freemason 'lodges' had grown to 126, and soon the secret order of the Brotherhood was spreading throughout Europe and the New World.

In fact, Freemasonry became so acceptable in the United States, that there is ample evidence to suggest that it was a highly influential force in framing the Constitution, even in designing the Great Seal of the United States, which is full of masonic symbols such as the All-Seeing Eye set within a triangle and the unfinished pyramid, which represents the unfinished temple of Solomon.

In recent years however, the freemasons or 'brotherhood', as they are sometimes known, have come in for a certain amount of criticism. This has arisen from growing suspicion about the continued intense secrecy surrounding the society's rituals and aims and a feeling that freemasons may put the interests of the society and their fellow members before that of say, the organization they work for. For instance there have been recommendations by a number of senior police chiefs, that policemen should not be members of any masonic lodge as this could present them with a conflict of interest in the course of their policework.

To become a freemason, a candidate must undergo a series of highly-secret ceremonies and tests. If an applicant is accepted by the lodge – and the vote must be unanimous – he must submit himself to the three-degree rituals.

Firstly, his head is covered, he is stripped of his clothes save for his underwear and shirt, and made to repeat numerous, often bizarre oaths. For the first degree of membership, 'the Entered Apprentice', the applicant's left breast, shoulder and arm are then bared and a rope is tied around his neck. For the second degree of membership, 'the Fellow Craft', the man's right breast, shoulder and arm are exposed. The rope is tied around his upper right arm. The third or 'Master Mason' degree also requires the candidate to be disrobed and blindfolded. The rope is then placed around the man's body three times.

In all three instances, the candidate must go through this procedure before he takes the oath for each degree. The Master Mason obligation, for instance, offers a blood-curdling penalty for violating the oath and failing in one's duties. It reads, in part, that a candidate 'will promise and swear that I will not write, print, stamp, stain, hew, cut, carve, indent, paint or engrave (masonic secrets) ... binding myself under no less penalty than to have my throat cut across, my tongue torn out by the roots, and my body buried in the rough sands of the sea at low water mark.'

Freemasonry, if nothing else, has a sense of the dramatic, but members insist it is a just society with secrets, not a secret society. But of all the fraternal groups, freemasons see the rituals and rites of their brotherhood as the essence of the organization's very being.